4846

MW00669227

NTERMEDIATE JAPAN.
A GRAMMAR AND WORKBOOK

termediate Japanese is designed for learners who have achieved a basic
roficiency and wish to progress to more complex language. Each unit
combines clear, concise grammar explanations with examples and
exercises to help build confidence and fluency.

The book is divided into two parts. Part 1 outlines fundamental
components of Japanese including particles, question words, verb types
and tense whereas Part 2 builds on this foundation by introducing
grammatical patterns organised by the task they achieve.

Features include:

- clear, accessible format
- jargon-free explanations of grammar
- many useful and culturally relevant examples
- abundant exercises with full answer key
- detailed index of grammar patterns.

Intermediate Japanese reviews the principal elements presented in its
sister volume, *Basic Japanese,* and introduces more complicated struc-
tures. Suitable for both classroom use and the independent learner, the
two books form a compendium of the essentials of Japanese grammar.

Takae Tsujioka is Teaching Assistant Professor in the Japanese
Language in the Department of East Asian Languages and Literatures at
the George Washington University.

Shoko Hamano is Professor of Japanese and International Affairs in the
Department of East Asian Languages and Literatures at the George
Washington University.

Other titles available in the Grammar Workbooks series are:

Basic Cantonese
Intermediate Cantonese

Basic Chinese
Intermediate Chinese

Basic German
Intermediate German

Basic Italian

Basic Irish
Intermediate Irish

Basic Japanese
Intermediate Japanese

Basic Korean
Intermediate Korean

Basic Polish
Intermediate Polish

Basic Russian
Intermediate Russian

Basic Spanish
Intermediate Spanish

Basic Welsh
Intermediate Welsh

Basic Yiddish

INTERMEDIATE JAPANESE: A GRAMMAR AND WORKBOOK

Takae Tsujioka and
Shoko Hamano

Routledge
Taylor & Francis Group

LONDON AND NEW YORK

First published 2012
by Routledge
2 Park Square, Milton Park, Abingdon, Oxon OX14 4RN

Simultaneously published in the USA and Canada
by Routledge
711 Third Avenue, New York, NY 10017

Routledge is an imprint of the Taylor & Francis Group, an informa business

British Library Cataloguing in Publication Data
A catalogue record for this book is available from the British Library

Library of Congress Cataloging in Publication Data
Tsujioka, Takae, 1970–
    Intermediate Japanese: a grammar and workbook/
    Takae Tsujioka and Shoko Hamano.
    p. cm.
    Includes index.
    1. Japanese language—Textbooks for foreign speakers—English.
    2. Japanese language—Grammar. 3. Japanese language—Spoken
Japanese. I. Hamano, Shoko, 1953– II. Title.
    PL539.5.E5T78 2012
    495.6'5—dc23
    2011033219

ISBN: 978-0-415-49858-6 (hbk)
ISBN: 978-0-415-49859-3 (pbk)

Typeset in Times New Roman and Univers
by Florence Production Ltd, Stoodleigh, Devon

MIX
Paper from
responsible sources
FSC® C004839

Printed and bound in Great Britain by the MPG Books Group

CONTENTS

Contents

PREFACE

As teachers with a combined teaching experience of over thirty years, we have always tried to take the students' perspective into account and highlight the functional aspect of the language as much as possible. At the same time, as trained linguists, we have always recognized the importance of providing accurate and consistent explanations of grammar for adult learners.

This book, like its companion book *Basic Japanese: A Grammar and Workbook*, is the result of these two aims. It explains the essential grammar of Japanese in an accessible yet linguistically accurate manner. The structure of the book also mirrors these considerations. The book is divided into two parts, focused on linguistic structure and function, respectively. We have also tried to carefully balance structure and function in each part.

Part 1 gives intermediate students the basic building blocks of the grammar, outlining fundamental components of Japanese, such as indeterminate pronouns, types of verbs, finer details of particles, tense, gender, and perspectives. These units are provided as comprehensive reference sections and contain cross references to many patterns that are introduced later in the book.

In Part 2, the introductory paragraph lays out the targeted tasks in a concise and friendly manner. The basic grammatical patterns are organized around these functional tasks. Here, the readers can learn a group of related patterns side by side looking at their subtle differences in usage so that they can not only understand the grammatical forms but also use them in a socially and culturally appropriate manner. Readers will find ample cross references between the units useful.

As far as possible, we have selected contextually related examples for each unit. That is, instead of introducing natural but disparate examples, we have aimed at weaving functionally related sentences and vocabulary into coherent pictures. It is hoped that this organization will not only facilitate the understanding of the grammatical patterns but also make it easier for readers to remember the examples as a group and be able to put them into use in real life.

Exercises at the end of each unit will check readers' comprehension and solidify their understanding. Although most of the vocabulary used in the exercises is recycled from the text section, a small dictionary may be useful from time to time. The answer keys to the exercises are provided at the end of the book.

The book also features three useful appendices on accent, basic conjugation patterns, and grammatical contexts for plain forms, て-forms, and stem forms, along with a glossary of grammatical terms and a detailed index of patterns and forms in alphabetical order.

We would like to thank the Routledge editors, Samantha Vale Noya and Isabelle Cheng, as well as the anonymous reviewers for their valuable comments. We would also like to thank our colleague, Wakana Kikuchi, for her charming illustrations. We also thank the team at Florence Production, for their careful handling of the complex manuscript. Any remaining errors are of course ours.

Finally, we would like to thank our families for their continuous support.

Notes on notation

In cross references, units in this book are referred to as "Unit 1," "Unit 2," and so on. Units in the companion volume *Basic Japanese: A Grammar and Workbook* are referred to as "*BJ* Unit 1," "*BJ* Units 2 and 3," and so on. *IJ* in Appendix C refers to this book.

In accordance with the current Japanese publishing standards, we represent the majority of numeric expressions using Arabic numerals, as in 1度 "one degree" 1つ "one item" and 1 月 "January." However, we will use *kanji* for some standard combinations that are usually represented with *kanji*, e.g. もう一度 "once more" and 一般的 "general."

We hope that this book will be used by independent learners as well as by students in formal classes. For this reason, we have annotated all the *kanji* in the examples with *furigana* (*ruby* letters over *kanji*). In addition, *furigana* are supplied for most Arabic numerals. However, we omitted *furigana* for lengthy Arabic numbers when it would otherwise take up too much space.

When marking the grammatical acceptability of sentences written in the Japanese script, we follow the Japanese tradition of using ○ (*maru*) for grammatical sentences and × (*batsu*) for ungrammatical or contextually inappropriate sentences.

The items that appear in the glossary are marked in small capital typeface when they appear in the text for the first time.

The following notation is used to refer to predicate types and grammatical categories:

P All types of predicates (i.e., verb, い-adjective, な-adjective/noun + the copula)
V Verb
A Both い-adjective and な-adjective
N Noun

- [V/A-stem] すぎる, for instance, means that this construction requires either a verb stem or an adjective stem.
- [Volitional V-plain non-past] ために means that this construction requires a volitional verb in its plain non-past form.
- [P-plain^(*da*-drop)] かもしれない means that this construction allows all types of predicates in their plain forms with a caveat that the plain non-past copula だ is dropped.

Part 1
Basic building blocks

UNIT 1

Indeterminate pronouns

Main target grammar in this unit

誰<small>だれ</small>も、誰<small>だれ</small>か、誰<small>だれ</small>でも、何人<small>なんにん</small>も、何人<small>なんにん</small>か、何人<small>なんにん</small>でも

In *Basic Japanese* Unit 7, we studied "question words" such as 誰<small>だれ</small>, 何<small>なに</small>, ど
ちら, どこ, and どう, which roughly correspond to English wh-words such
as "who," "what," "which," "where," and "how." Although often thought
of as question words, English wh-words are used not only in questions but
also in concessive statements. For example:

No matter how convenient cell phones are, she will not buy one.

The Japanese counterparts of English wh-words also appear in concessive
statements like the above sentence. In addition, they take on the meanings
of such English words as "every," "some," or "any," depending on the
PARTICLE with which they combine, and are better called **INDETER-
MINATE PRONOUNS**. In this unit we will study various non-question-word
uses of Japanese indeterminate pronouns.

Japanese indeterminate pronouns

A list of common Japanese indeterminate pronouns is given below. We
mark the location of an **ACCENT**, a significant fall in the pitch level within
a word, with the backslash (\). We do this because accent is consequential
in the discussion of indeterminate pronouns, as shown later. (*See*
Appendix A for the explanation of accent.)

誰(だ\れ)   "who"
何(な\に or な\ん)   "what"
ど\れ   "which one"

3

ど\ちら	"which option"; "which way" [**POLITE**]
ど\っち	"which option"; "which way"
ど\こ	"where"
い\つ	"when"
ど\のN	"which (+ noun)"
ど\んなN	"what type of (+ noun)"
な\ぜ	"why"
ど\う	"how"
ど\うして	"why"
い\くら	"how much"
い\くつ	"how many"

Note that these indeterminate pronouns are all accented on the first syllable.

In addition, **INDETERMINATE QUANTIFIERS**, combinations of 何^{なん} and a **COUNTER**, are also accented on the first syllable. Some examples are given here:

何人 （な\んにん）	"how many people"
何台 （な\んだい）	"how many vehicles"
何匹 （な\んびき）	"how many animals"
何回 （な\んかい）	"how many times"
何才 （な\んさい）	"how old"
何年 （な\んねん）	"how many years/which year"

Use of indeterminate pronouns in the sense of "every"

All indeterminate pronouns except for なぜ "why" can combine with the particle も. Accented combinations of an indeterminate pronoun and も mean "every item in the category." However, 何^{なに} "what" does not have this option.

誰も(だ\れも)	"everyone"
ど\こも	"all places"
ど\れも	"every item"
ど\ちらも	"both"
ど\の商品^{しょうひん}も	"every product"
ど\んな商品^{しょうひん}も	"every kind of product"
い\つも	"always"

These expressions can appear either with a positive or a negative ending.

新製品は、ど\ちらも売りにくかった。
"As for the new products, both were difficult to sell."

新製品は、ど\ちらも売りやすくなかった。
"As for the new products, both were not easy to sell."

Used as a **SUBJECT** or **OBJECT**, these expressions usually appear without the structure particle が or を. However, が and を remain after だ\れも "everyone."

その広告は日本人のだ\れもが知っている。
"Every Japanese person knows that advertisement."

Meaning-oriented particles (*see BJ* Unit 5) such as から are obligatory and must precede も.

ど\の取引先からも注文が来ました。
"Merchandise orders came from every client."

When combined with the particle も, some indeterminate pronouns turn unaccented. These unaccented combinations are used to negate a statement with regard to an entire class of people or things and must appear with a negative **PREDICATE** within the same clause.

誰も(〜ない)   "not … anyone" = "nobody"
何も(〜ない)   "not … anything" = "nothing"
どこも(〜ない)   "not … anywhere" = "nowhere"

In this pattern, the structure particles が and を are dropped.

誰も何も買いませんでした。
"Nobody bought anything."

As in the case of accented versions, the meaning-oriented particles such as から are obligatory and must appear before も.

どこからも注文が来ませんでした。
"Merchandise orders did not come from anywhere."

Use of indeterminate pronouns in the sense of "some"

Indeterminate pronouns can also be combined with the particle か. The particle か, which functions as a question marker at the end of a sentence, here signifies that the object is unidentified. For instance, だれか means "unidentified person," hence "somebody." When combined with か, all indeterminate pronouns keep the accent on the initial syllable.

誰か(だ\れか)	"somebody"
何か(な\にか or な\んか)	"something"
ど\こか	"somewhere"
ど\れか	"one item"
ど\ちらか	"one of the two"
い\つか	"some day"
い\くつか	"a few"
い\くらか	"some amount"

Again, the structure particles が and を are optional, whereas the meaning-oriented particles are obligatory. However, unlike も, か combined with an indeterminate pronoun precedes all additional particles.

誰か(が)受付にいます。
"There is someone at the receptionist counter."

どちらか(を)説明してください。
"Please explain either one of them."

どこかでその広告を見ました。
"I saw the advertisement somewhere."

Note that the above sentences containing indeterminate pronouns are not to be confused with questions. To turn them into questions, you need the sentence-final question marker か or the rising intonation pattern.

誰か受付にいますか。
"Is there someone at the receptionist desk?"

誰か受付にいます?↗
"Is there someone at the receptionist desk?"

You can narrow down the category of the unidentified object by adding another **NOUN PHRASE**.

誰<ruby>だれ</ruby>かお<ruby>客きゃく</ruby>さんが<ruby>待ま</ruby>っています。
"Some customer is waiting."

誰<ruby>だれ</ruby>か<ruby>知し</ruby>らない<ruby>人ひと</ruby>が<ruby>会議室かいぎしつ</ruby>にいます。
"There is someone I don't know in the conference room."

Use of indeterminate pronouns in the sense of free choice "any"

Indeterminate pronouns when combined with でも are equivalent to such English expressions as "whoever," "whatever," and "wherever," or expressions containing "any" that indicate a free choice. Sentences containing these expressions mean that the statement applies to any member of the class. Indeterminate pronouns in these expressions can be accented or unaccented.

誰<ruby>だれ</ruby>でも	"anybody," "whoever"
何<ruby>なん</ruby>でも	"anything," "whatever"
どこでも	"anywhere," "wherever"
どれでも	"any one of the items," "whichever"
どちらでも	"either of the two," "whichever"
いつでも	"any time," "whenever"
いくつでも	"any number of items," "however many"
いくらでも	"any amount," "however much"

Here is an example sentence:

この<ruby>商品しょうひん</ruby>はいつでも<ruby>買か</ruby>えます。
"You can buy this product any time."

The meaning-oriented particles, if used, must precede でも.

<ruby>返品へんぴん</ruby>したい<ruby>時とき</ruby>にはどの<ruby>店みせ</ruby>へでも<ruby>返かえ</ruby>せます。
"When you want to return it, you can return it to any store."

<ruby>新あたら</ruby>しい<ruby>携帯けいたい</ruby>は<ruby>世界中せかいじゅう</ruby>どこででも<ruby>使つか</ruby>える。
"You can use the new cell phone anywhere in the world."

Indeterminate quantifiers with も, か, or でも

The combination of an indeterminate quantifier and も has the sense that the speaker considers the amount large.

何億年も	"many hundreds of millions of years"
何万人も	"many tens of thousands of people"
何千万円も	"many tens of millions of yen"
何十年も	"many tens of years"

新製品は、何百回もテストしました。
"We have tested the new product many hundreds of times."

何十回も会社に電話をしましたが、出ませんでした。
"I called the company many tens of times, but they did not answer the phone."

The combination of an indeterminate quantifier and か means an approximate number.

何百万匹か	"some millions of creatures"
何十万冊か	"some hundreds of thousands of books"
何万人か	"some tens of thousands of people"
何百回か	"some hundreds of times"

何人か受付で待っています。
"A few people are waiting at the receptionist counter."

サイトに何十万人かアクセスしました。
"Some hundreds of thousands of people accessed the website."

The combination of an indeterminate quantifier and でも means that the outcome is the same regardless of the quantity. (*See also* Unit 18 on CONDITIONALS.)

何億年でも	"no matter how many hundreds of millions of years"
何万人でも	"no matter how many tens of thousands of people"
何千万円でも	"no matter how many tens of millions of yen"
何十年でも	"no matter how many tens of years"

Here are a couple of example sentences:

出るまで何十回でも電話します。

"I will call them any number of times until they answer the phone."

何万円でも払います。

"I will pay no matter how many tens of thousands of yen it may cost."

Exercise 1.1

Provide answers matching the English translations.

1. A: 何を買いましたか。

   B: <u>何も買いませんでした</u>。"I didn't buy anything."

2. A: 誰に聞きましたか。

   B: <u>誰にも聞きませんでした</u>。 "I didn't ask anyone."

3. A: どこに行きましたか。

   B: <u>どこにも行きませんでした</u>。 "I didn't go anywhere."

Exercise 1.2

Fill in the blanks with the appropriate indeterminate pronoun. You can
check the meaning of each dialog in the Key to exercises.

1. A: 午前中に(誰)か学生が来ましたか。

   B: ええ、大学院生が1人来ましたよ。

2. A: 最近(何)かおもしろい映画を見ましたか。

   B: ええ、「マジック」という映画を見ました。

3. A: (どこ)か安い靴屋を知りませんか。

B: そうですね。駅前のスーパーにも安い靴がありますよ。

Exercise 1.3

Complete the following **YES-NO QUESTIONS** and answers by filling in the blanks with the appropriate particles. You can check the meaning of each dialog in the Key to exercises.

1. A: 誰(か)電話に出た?

B: ううん、誰(も)出なかった。

2. A: 誰(か)(から)電話があった?

B: ううん、誰(から)(も)なかった。

3. A: 日曜日にどこ(か)(に)行きましたか。

B: いいえ、どこ(に)(も)行きませんでした。

Exercise 1.4

Suppose that you feel very lethargic. Following the example, complete the sentences, and translate them into English.

Example

仕事はたくさんありますが、何**もしたくありません**。

"I have a lot of work, but I don't feel like doing anything."

1. コーヒーも紅茶もありますが、どちら*も飲みたくありません*

2. 部屋にテレビはありますが、何*も見たくありません*。

3. 外はいい天気ですが、どこ*も行きたくありません*

4. 友だちが来るんですが、本当は誰*にも会いたくありません*。

Exercise 1.5

Choose the appropriate particle. You can check the meaning of each sentence in the Key to exercises.

1. 2つ要りますから、どちら{か/(も)/でも}買います。

2. お金があまりないから、どちら{(か)/も/でも}しか買えません。

3. とても高かったので、どちら{か/(も)/でも}買いませんでした。

4. どちら{か/も/(でも)}いいですから、どちらか買って下さい。

Exercise 1.6

Fill in the blanks with an appropriate verb and translate the completed passage.

Example

あの映画は大好きだから、**何度でも見ます**。

"I love that movie, so I watch it any number of times."

1. 加藤さんは、古いカーペットが好きです。古いのをさがして、どこへでも＿＿＿＿＿＿。

2. 木村さんは、いろいろな地図を集めるのが趣味です。古本屋にある時は、1度に何枚でも＿＿＿＿＿＿。

3. 漢字は難しいから、何度でも＿＿＿＿＿＿、覚えます。

4. 田中先生の研究室は、今マーケットリサーチをしています。たくさんデータが要りますから、メンバーは、アンケートに答えてくれる人をさがして毎日何十人にでも＿＿＿＿＿＿。

UNIT 2
Types of verbs

> ### Main target grammar in this unit
>
> **Eventive** versus **stative** verbs, **action** versus **change-of-state** verbs, **volitional** versus **non-volitional** verbs, **transitive** versus **intransitive** verbs

There is a huge difference between the two English sentences "I stopped it" and "I stopped." This is because the verb "stop" in the first sentence is a **TRANSITIVE VERB** whereas "stop" in the second sentence is an **INTRANSITIVE VERB**. Distinctions such as this have various grammatical consequences. For example, English passive sentences can only contain transitive verbs. Many Japanese grammatical constructions also must refer to verb types such as these. In this unit, we will provide an overview of the basic Japanese verb types that are mentioned throughout this book. These verb types will also be noted in some headings in the shortened form of "Action V," "Volitional V," etc.

Eventive versus stative verbs

Verbs can be classified according to whether they describe an event or state. One easy method to accomplish this is to ask the question "What happens next?". You can answer the question with an **EVENTIVE VERB**, but not with a **STATIVE VERB**.

田中さんがピアノをひきます。　　[eventive verb]
"Mr. Tanaka will play the piano."

ピアノがあります。　　[stative verb]
"There is a piano."

Stative verbs show many special grammatical properties. For example, the object of a lexical stative verb is marked with が instead of を (*see also* Unit 3 and *BJ* Unit 5).

ピアノのひき方が分かりません。
"I don't know how to play the piano."

Endings such as [V-て] いる that express ASPECT are also sensitive to the eventuality of verbs. The basic function of [V-て] いる is to modify eventive verbs and describe stable or sustained conditions.

私は、田中さんの演奏を聞いています。
"I am listening to Mr. Tanaka's performance."

Stative verbs, which inherently describe states, usually do not have [V-て] いる counterparts.

× ピアノがあっている (○ある)。
(*intended*: "There is a piano.")

In rare cases where [V-て] いる is added to a stative verb, it does not make as marked a difference in the meaning as when it is added to an eventive verb.

ピアノが聞こえる。
"The piano sound is audible."

ピアノが聞こえている。
"The piano sound is audible (right now)."

See Unit 8 for more details on [V-て] いる.

Action versus change-of-state verbs

Eventive verbs can be further divided into ACTION VERBS and CHANGE-OF-STATE VERBS. Here, the relevant concept of "change" is whether the **subject** of a verb undergoes a change. Notice that the change-of-state verb 出来る "complete" in the following example entails that the subject

協奏曲 "concerto" changes its status from "not completed" to "completed":

協奏曲が出来ました。　　[change-of-state verb]
"A concerto was completed."

Similarly, the verb あがる "get up" in the following example necessarily means that the subject 指揮者 "conductor" changes location, ending up "on the stage." This type of verb is known as a **CHANGE-OF-LOCATION VERB**.

指揮者がステージにあがりました。[change-of-location verb]
"The conductor got up on the stage."

In contrast, the subject of an action verb does not undergo a grammatically meaningful change. For example, consider the following sentence:

田中さんが走りました。　　[action verb]
"Mr. Tanaka ran."

Mr. Tanaka might get sweaty and eventually lose weight as a result of running, but it is also possible that he will not. In other words, the action verb 走る "run" does not entail changes. Similarly, Mr. Tanaka might move around, but the verb 走る does not require him to end up in a different location from where he started. He could run in circles or run on a treadmill.

These meaning differences also have grammatical consequences. For example, whereas change-of-location verbs have a specified destination that is marked with the particle に "to," action verbs do not. If you want to add an end point of movement, you must use the particle まで "until" instead.

指揮者が**ステージに**あがりました。[change-of-location verb]
"The conductor got up on the stage."

田中さんが**ステージまで**(×に)走りました。[action verb]
"Mr. Tanaka ran to the stage."

Another important grammatical consequence of the contrast is the differing interpretation of the aspectual ending [V-て] いる. When combined with いる, action verbs have the action-in-progress reading (introduced in *BJ* Unit 6). In contrast, verbs that specify a change in the subject have the **RESULTANT CONTINUATIVE** meaning, which highlights the end result of an event rather than a process (*see* Unit 8). Observe the meaning differences between the two examples below:

田中さんが走っています。　　　　[action verb]
"Mr. Tanaka is running."

協奏曲が出来ています。　　　　[change-of-state verb]
"A concerto has been completed."

When a verb describes a change that takes place over a span of time rather than an instantaneous change, the action-in-progress reading is also available, rendering the sentence ambiguous, as in the following:

指揮者がステージにあがっています。 [change-of-location verb]
"The conductor is up on the stage."
"The conductor is getting up onto the stage [by climbing the stairs, etc.]"

Volitional versus non-volitional verbs

VOLITIONALITY has to do with whether or not one has the will or volition to do something. An action verb always has a **VOLITIONAL SUBJECT**, whereas the subject of a stative verb is usually non-volitional.

テレビでコンサートを見ました。　[volitional]
"I saw a concert on TV."

楽譜の読み方が分かりません。　　[non-volitional]
"I don't know how to read the music score."

The subject of a change-of-state/location verb is mostly non-volitional.

歌が終わりました。　　　　　　[non-volitional]
"The song ended."

楽譜がかばんに入りました。　　[non-volitional]
"The music score fit into the bag."

However, the subject of a change-of-state/location verb can be volitional if it is animate.

√ 楽団の指揮者が引退しました。　　[volitional]

"The conductor of the orchestra retired."

√ ベルが鳴ったからコンサートホールに入りました。 [volitional]

"We went inside the concert hall because the bell rang."

Many grammatical constructions exclude non-volitional verbs. For example, non-volitional verbs do not occur in the [V-stem] たい-form, **POTENTIAL FORMS**, or **VOLITIONAL FORMS** (*see BJ* Units 15, 16, and 19, respectively).

× オーケストラが見えたい。　　cf. オーケストラが見たい。

(*intended*: "I want to be able to see the orchestra.")

× バッハが分かれる。　　cf. バッハが分かる。

(*intended*: "I can understand Bach.")

× コンサートがあろう。　　cf. コンサートをしよう。

(*intended*: "Let's have a concert.")

Similarly, only volitional verbs may be used in purpose phrases (*see* Unit 13).

√ 音楽を勉強するためにウィーンへ行った。

"I went to Vienna in order to study music."

× 音楽の勉強が出来るためにウィーンへ行った。

(*intended*: "I went to Vienna in order to be able to study music.")

Volitional and non-volitional verbs do not form exclusive classes. An identical form may function sometimes as a volitional verb and sometimes as a non-volitional verb. For instance, the verb いる in the sense of "there exist (animate)" is incompatible with the potential construction.

× このクラスには10人いられる。

(*intended*: "Ten people are able to be in this class.")

However, it can occur in the potential and volitional forms when it is used in the sense of "stay."

いつまでウィーンにいられるの?
"Until when can you stay in Vienna?"

もう少し長くいようよ。
"Let's stay a little longer."

Transitive versus intransitive verbs

A transitive verb occurs with a subject and an object. On the other hand, an intransitive verb only occurs with a subject.

私がバイオリンを買った。   [transitive verb]
"I bought a violin."

バイオリンが壊れた。   [intransitive verb]
"The violin broke."

In English, many verbs are used both transitively and intransitively as in the following:

The conductor **began** the performance.   [transitive]
The performance **began**.   [intransitive]

The transitive "begin" is an action verb whose subject volitionally induces a change. On the other hand, the intransitive "begin" is a change-of-state verb whose subject undergoes what appears to be a spontaneous change.

The corresponding Japanese verbs have closely related but different forms.

指揮者が演奏を始めた。   [transitive]
"The conductor began the performance."

演奏が始まった。   [intransitive]
"The performance began."

17

Japanese has a large number of transitive-intransitive verb pairs such as 始める and 始まる. The following table gives some representative samples. The intransitive members are either change-of-state or change-of-location verbs.

Transitive verb	Intransitive verb
始_{はじ}める "begin"	始_{はじ}まる "begin"
開_あける "open"	開_あく "open"
閉_しめる "close"	閉_しまる "close"
つける "turn on"	つく "turn on"
消_けす "turn off"	消_きえる "go off"
出_だす "submit, serve"	出_でる "come out, be served"
入_いれる "put in"	入_{はい}る "enter"
切_きる "cut"	切_きれる "be cut"
壊_{こわ}す "break"	壊_{こわ}れる "break"
届_{とど}ける "deliver"	届_{とど}く "be delivered"
のせる "put on"	のる "get on"
なおす "fix"	なおる "be fixed"
見_みつける "find"	見_みつかる "be found"
かわかす "dry	かわく "get dry"
ぬらす "wet"	ぬれる "get wet"
落_おとす "drop"	落_おちる "drop, fall"
する* "do, render"	なる "become"

*See Unit 14 for the use of する "do" and なる "become" as a transitive-intransitive pair in describing changes of various kinds.

Even when describing their own willful accomplishment, Japanese speakers tend to favor intransitive members over their transitive counterparts if they feel that the outcome was not completely under their control. For example, finally finding his misplaced key after an hour's search, a Japanese speaker might say:

√ 良かった。鍵が見つかった。
"Good. The key turned up."

The transitive counterpart in such a situation sounds quite odd.

× 良かった。鍵を見つけた。
(*intended*: "Good. I found the key.")

Distinguishing between a transitive and an intransitive member may seem challenging at first, but there are a couple of tips that can help you tell them apart.

Tip 1
Given a pair of transitive and intransitive verbs, the one ending with す is always the **transitive** member. (Remember this by associating the sound *su* with the prototypical transitive verb する "do.")

Tip 2
Given a pair of transitive and intransitive verbs, the one ending with an *a*-row syllable plus る is always the **intransitive** member. (Remember this by associating the sound *aru* with the prototypical intransitive verb ある "be.")

Exercise 2.1

Consider the meaning of the verb in bold and mark an action verb as [AV], a change-of-state verb as [CSV], and a change-of-location verb as [CLV]. You can check the meaning of each sentence in the Key to exercises.

1. 家の前にタクシーが**止まり**ました。
2. 駅まで**歩き**ましょう。
3. ドアが**閉まり**ました。

4. このワインボトルは、手で**開ける**ことができます。

5. パソコンの電源が**切れ**ました。

6. 先月、**結婚**しました。

7. 明日はどこに**行き**ましょうか。

8. 質問がある人は、手を**あげて**下さい。

9. 今学期は、成績が**あがって**うれしいです。

10. アラスカに行ってオーロラを**見ました**。

Exercise 2.2

Determine if each bold-face verb in Exercise 2.1 has a volitional or non-volitional subject. (Note that most of the sentences in Exercise 2.1 have an implied subject.)

Exercise 2.3

Select the transitive member for each pair of verbs.

1. 閉まる　/　閉める　　　"close"

2. 開ける　/　開く　　　　"open"

3. 消える　/　消す　　　　"turn off"

4. 止める　/　止まる　　　"stop"

5. 直す　　/　直る　　　　"fix"

6. 帰る　　/　返す　　　　"return"

7. 変える　/　変わる　　　"change"

8. 起こす　/　起きる　　　"wake up"

9. 始まる　/　始める　　　"begin"

10. 落ちる　/　落とす　　　"drop"

Exercise 2.4

2
Types of
verbs

Choose the appropriate form. You can check the meaning of each sentence in the Key to exercises.

1. 寝る前にテレビを{消して/消えて}ね。
2. 夏休みが{始める/始まる}のはいつですか。
3. 寒いから、ヒーターを{つけ/つき}ましょう。
4. 風邪が{治して/治って}良かったですね。
5. この作文はもう一度書き{直して/直って}下さい。
6. ケーキを4つに{切って/切れて}食べた。
7. 私が7時になっても起きなかったら、{起こして/起きて}ね。
8. 日本では、ゴミを燃えるゴミと燃えないゴミに分けて{出す/出る}。

Exercise 2.5

Fill in the blanks with an appropriately conjugated verb from the parentheses. Do not use the same verb twice. You can check the meaning of each sentence in the Key to exercises.

1. (開く　開ける)

   このビン、ふたがかたくて＿＿＿＿んだけど、陽子ちゃん、＿＿＿＿られる?

2. (見える　見る)

   花火を＿＿＿＿ために来たけど、高い建物が多くて、ぜんぜん＿＿＿＿なかったね。

3. (出る　出す)

   ねえ、ジロー(＝犬の名前)が外に＿＿＿＿たがっているから、ちょっと＿＿＿＿やって。

4. (止まる　止める)

   A novice skier at a ski resort …

   「きゃー、＿＿＿＿ないよ! 誰か私を＿＿＿＿!!」

21

UNIT 3

More on particles

Main target grammar in this unit

コンピューターが要る、先生に聞く、音楽を聞く、友達と話す、友達に話す、家を出る、駅に着く、ピアノのひき方

As discussed in *BJ* Unit 5, the prototypical function of the particle を is to mark the direct object of a transitive verb. An を-marked phrase in Japanese usually corresponds to the direct object of a transitive verb in English, as in "John ate a **hamburger**." However, this is not always the case. Sometimes, the particle を is not used where English speakers would expect it. For example, the Japanese phrases corresponding to the bold parts in "I like **dogs**," "I met **the new professor**," and "Nancy married **an investment banker**" are each marked by a particle other than を. Conversely, を sometimes appears where an English speaker would not expect it. For example, を is used to mark the phrases corresponding to the bold parts in "I went **through the park**" and "I graduated **from college** in 1992." In this unit, we focus on such instances that require special attention.

The use of が instead of を

The particle が, not を, marks the object of an adjective or stative verb (*see* Unit 2).

私は邦画があまり好きじゃありません。　　[adjective]
"I don't like Japanese movies very much."

私は漢英辞典の使い方が分かりません。　　[stative verb]
"I don't know how to use a Kanji-English dictionary."

The object of the [V-stem] たい pattern (*BJ* Unit 15) or a potential form (*BJ* Unit 16) is optionally marked by が because of the stative meaning associated with wish or ability.

ピアノ{が/を}ひきたいです。 [V-たい pattern]
"I want to play the piano."

ピアノ{が/を}ひけます。 [potential verb]
"I can play the piano."

With these patterns, you can use either が or を without creating a substantial difference in meaning. However, adding an element that increases the sense of volitional control can tip the balance in favor of を. For instance, if the verbal **SUFFIX** がる "behave as if" (*BJ* Unit 15) is attached to たい, the stative meaning is reduced, and the object must again be marked by を.

妹_{いもうと}はピアノをひきたがります。
"My sister is eager to play the piano."

The use of に instead of を

The target of an interpersonal transaction is marked by に. Do not use を in cases such as the following:

プロジェクトについては山本_{やまもと}さんに聞_きいて下_{くだ}さい。
"Please ask Mr. Yamamoto regarding the project."

鈴本先生_{すずきせんせい}にお歳暮_{せいぼ}をお送_{おく}りしました。
"I sent Prof. Yamamoto a year-end gift."

アルバイト先_{さき}に連絡_{れんらく}した方_{ほう}がいいよ。
"You should contact your part-time job employer."

友人_{ゆうじん}が私_{わたし}に車_{くるま}を売_うってくれた。
"My friend sold me his car."

Similarly, the human target of an emotion expressed with an adjective is
marked by に.

父は 妹 に甘い。

"My father spoils my sister."

先生は 私 にとても親切にして下さいました。

"My teacher was very kind to me."

The use of と instead of を

When a verb expresses a reciprocal action between two equal parties, the
non-subject party is marked by と.

吉田さんは銀行員と結婚しました。

"Ms. Yoshida married a banker."

昨日彼氏とけんかしちゃったの。 (*See* Unit 19 for しちゃう)

"I ended up having a fight with my boyfriend."

The particle と also appears with adjectives that describe a reciprocal
relationship.

藤原さんは佐藤さんと親しい。

"Ms. Fujiwara is close to Mr. Sato."

Some verbs that express reciprocal actions also occur with に, but with a
reduced sense of reciprocity. For instance, of the following pair of sentences containing 会う "meet," the と version implies that Mr. Takahashi,
the non-subject participant, willfully participated and was equally
involved in the action. The に version does not necessarily imply such
a commitment on the part of Mr. Takahashi and can be interpreted as a
description of an accidental encounter.

東京駅で高橋さんと会いました。

"I met up with Ms. Takahashi at the Tokyo station."

東京駅で高橋さんに会いました。

"I ran into/met Ms. Takahashi at the Tokyo station."

Note also that you may not use を with reciprocal 会う, whereas you must use を with non-reciprocal 見る "see, watch."

東京駅で向かいのプラットホームに高橋さんを見ました。
"I saw Ms. Takahashi on the platform across from where I was at the Tokyo station."

Special use of を

The particle を was introduced in *BJ* Unit 5 as the structure particle that marks the object of a transitive verb. However, を sometimes appears with an intransitive verb. First, を marks the point of departure.

午前6時に家を出ました。 [point of departure]
"I left home at 6 a.m."

大学を卒業してから、どうするんですか。
"What are you going to do after graduating from college?"

新大阪を10時に出る新幹線は１２時１６分に品川に着きます。
"The bullet train that departs Shin-Osaka at 10 arrives in Shinagawa at 12:16."

The destination, on the other hand, is marked by に (*see BJ* Unit 5).

大学に着きました。 [arrival point]
"I arrived at the university."

The particle を also marks the path of movement of a motion verb.

公園を通って、行きましょう。 [path of movement]
"Let's go through the park."

危ないから、歩道を歩いた方がいいですよ。
"It's dangerous, so you should walk on the sidewalk."

あの橋を渡って、すぐですよ。
"After crossing that bridge, it's right there."

Note, however, that the distance that one covers is expressed with a
NUMERAL QUANTIFIER (*see BJ* Unit 9) and does not bear a particle.

今朝は、 ３キロ(×を)走りました。
"This morning, I ran 3 km."

The use of の in modifiers of verbal nouns

Like regular nouns, **VERBAL NOUNS** such as 勉強 "studying," テニス
"tennis," and 旅行 "trip" (*see BJ* Unit 3) can be modified by a noun, a い/
な-adjective, or a verb.

２週間の旅行	"two-week trip"
大事な旅行	"important trip"
面白い旅行	"interesting trip"
去年した旅行	"trip I did last year"

In addition, verbal nouns can be modified by various noun phrases that
are closely related to their meanings. For instance, given the following
sentence,

私が友達と新幹線で九州へ旅行します。
"I will travel to Kyushu by the bullet train with my friends."

you can create a noun phrase such as the following:

私の友達との新幹線での九州への旅行
"my trip to Kyushu by the bullet train with my friends"

Note that the meaning-oriented particles と, へ, and で (*see BJ* Unit 5) that
appear in the sentence show up in the corresponding noun phrases with
the particle の.

新幹線での旅行	"trip by the bullet train"
九州への旅行	"trip to Kyushu"
友達との旅行	"trip with my friends"

Note also that, even though に is a viable goal particle in a sentence, it cannot be used in a noun phrase. Use へ instead.

九州{へ/に}旅行します。
"I will travel to Kyushu."

× 九州にの旅行
"trip to Kyushu"

The subject particle が is replaced by の.

私の旅行　　　　　　　"my trip"

Similarly, the direct object of a transitive sentence is marked by の in a corresponding noun phrase.

地理を勉強します。　　　"I will study geography."
地理の勉強　　　　　　　"studying of geography"

This same pattern is observed with the construction [V-stem] 方, which derives nouns meaning "how to ..." from verbs.

歩きます "walk"　　→　　歩き方 "how to walk"
食べます "eat"　　→　　食べ方 "how to eat"

Such derived nouns are modified in the same manner as verbal nouns.

弟がインドへ行きます。 →　弟のインドへの行き方
"My brother will go to India."　"my brother's way of going to India"

私がすしを食べます。　　→　　私のすしの食べ方
"I eat *sushi*."　　　　　　"my way of eating *sushi*"

Here are some example sentences showing how to use such noun phrases:

弟のインドへの行き方はとてもユニークだった。
"How my brother went to India was very unique."

私のすしの食べ方をよく見て下さい。
"Please pay attention to how I eat *sushi*."

27

Exercise 3.1

Choose between が and を. If both are possible, indicate that. You can check the meaning of each sentence in the Key to exercises.

1. どんな映画{が/を}見たい?
2. 霧で前{が/を}よく見えません。
3. 彼女は自分のこと{が/を}言いたがらない。
4. 私は彼の気持ちを理解すること{が/を}出来なかった。
5. けっきょく大事なこと{が/を}話せなかった。

Exercise 3.2

Choose between に and と. You can check the meaning of each sentence in the Key to exercises.

1. 何か問題があったら、すぐ私{に/と}言って下さい。
2. 藤原さんは佐藤さん{に/と}大学院時代に友だちになった。
3. 全員{に/と}メールしたんですが、返事はこれだけです。
4. 子どもの時、弟{に/と}よくけんかをしました。
5. 両親は、私{に/と}きびしかった。

Exercise 3.3

Choose from に, と, and を. You can check the meaning of each sentence in the Key to exercises.

1. 日本人{に/と/を}結婚しましたが、国籍はカナダです。
2. その子は私{に/と/を}じっと見ました。
3. 交番で警察官{に/と/を}道を聞いた。
4. 東京の真ん中で高校時代の友だち{に/と/を}出会った。
5. 妹も私も夕飯のテーブルをかこんで両親{に/と/を}よく話します。

Exercise 3.4

Fill in the blanks with the appropriate particle. **Do not** use は or も. If none is allowed, write Ø.

1. 鳥たちが空 (　　) 飛んで行く。

    "Birds are flying across the sky."

2. 鳥たちは海(　　) 渡って日本(　　) 来る。

    "The birds come to Japan flying across the ocean."

3. 鳥たちは陸(　　) 離れてから１日に平均２００キロ(　　) 飛ぶ。

    "After leaving the shore, the birds fly 200 km a day on average."

Exercise 3.5

Following the example, formulate noun phrases from the following sentences.

Example

ピアノをひきます。　　　　→　　　ピアノのひき方
"I will play the piano."　　　　　"how to play the piano"

1. 楽譜を読みます。　　　　→　　　_____

    "I read the music score."

2. 先生が子供を扱います。　→　　　_____

    "The teacher handles the children."

3. 日本で英語を教えます。　→　　　_____

    "They teach English in Japan."

UNIT 4

Tense and timing

The Japanese language distinguishes between two basic **TENSES**: non-past
and past. In this unit we will study how to make use of these two tenses.
(For the explanation of how to conjugate the predicates for non-past and
past, *see* Appendix B and *BJ* Unit 6.) In addition, we will study the issues
of timing between the events in the main and **DEPENDENT CLAUSES** (*see*
BJ Unit 4).

Non-past tense

Non-past tense is also known as present tense, but its use is not limited to
present events or conditions. **STATIVE PREDICATES** (*see* Unit 2 and *BJ*
Units 3 and 5) in non-past tense express present or general conditions.

屋根の上に猫がいる。　　　[present condition]
"There is a cat on the rooftop."

犬も猫も大好きだ。　　　[general condition]
"I like both dogs and cats very much."

Eventive verbs (*see* Unit 2) in non-past tense express general or habitual
conditions as well as future or yet unrealized events.

父は毎朝、犬と公園を散歩する。　　　[habitual]
"Every morning, my father takes a walk in the park with our dog."

夕方、犬をペット病院に連れて行く。　　　[future event]

"I will/am going to take the dog to a pet clinic in the evening."

Although the **PROGRESSIVE CONSTRUCTION** "be …-ing" is sometimes used in colloquial English in order to talk about intention, this usage is not available for the Japanese progressive construction (*see* Unit 8). Use the ordinary non-past tense, as in the last sentence in the example above.

Past tense

In the case of action verbs (*see* Unit 2 and *BJ* Unit 3), the past-tense marker indicates whether or not the action took place in the past.

朝、犬と散歩したので、夕方は、散歩しなかった。

"Because I took a walk with the dog in the morning, I did not take a walk in the evening."

In the case of stative predicates (*see* Unit 2 and *BJ* Units 3 and 5), the past-tense marker indicates whether or not the condition held true in the past.

子猫の毛はやわらかかった。子犬の毛はやわらかくなかった。

"The kitten's fur was soft. The puppy's fur was not soft."

Special use of the past tense

The past tense forms of stative predicates have an extra function. In the process of verifying information about a present or future condition, they can signify that the speaker believes to have heard the assertions before.

A: この犬の名前、何だった?

"What did you say was the name of this dog?"

B: クロだよ。

"It's Kuro."

A: ああ、そうだったね。

"Oh, that's right. (You said that.)"

31

Note that the tense of the reply need not be in the past tense if the respondent can firmly confirm the veracity of the assertion.

A: 病院の予約は、今日じゃなかったよね。
"They said that the appointment is not for today, right?"

B: うん。{今日じゃなかった/今日じゃない}。
"Right. (They said) it's not today."

Do not reply with past tense forms if your personal information is being verified.

A: お名前は、杉田さんでしたね。
"You said your name is Sugita, right?"

B: はい、そうです。杉田です。
"Yes, my name is Sugita."

Another special use of the past-tense marker involves expressions of gratitude or apology, such as the following (*see also BJ* Unit 25):

すみません   "I am sorry (for the inconvenience)"
ありがとうございます   "thank you"
失礼します   "excuse me"
お疲れさまです   "(thank you for) a hard day's work"
ご苦労様です   "you've completed a challenging task"

These non-past expressions mean that the interaction for which the feeling is expressed is still in progress. Their past-tense counterparts are used if the interaction was completed some time ago or has come to a conclusion. For instance, when an attendant receives money from a customer in exchange for some service, he first says ありがとうございます, but when the customer is leaving the store, he says ありがとうございました.

Tense in dependent clauses

In English, tense-marking is speaker oriented. That is, the past or the non-past is determined relative to the point of the utterance. This is true regardless of whether the event is in the main or the dependent clause.

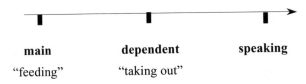

The timing of speaking, the main event, and the dependent event are schematically shown on a timeline below.

I **fed** the dog before I **took** him out.

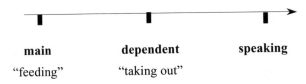

I will **feed** the dog before I **take** him out.

In Japanese, too, the tense of the MAIN CLAUSE is determined relative to the point when the speaker utters the sentence. However, the tense of the dependent clause is usually determined relative to the main clause, not the point of the utterance. That is, if the dependent-clause event precedes the main-clause event, the dependent clause appears in the past tense. The speaker's position is irrelevant.

トレーニングを受けた犬は静かにしているだろう。
"Those dogs that have gone through the training will remain quiet."

トレーニングを受けた犬は静かにしていた。
"Those dogs that had gone through the training remained quiet."

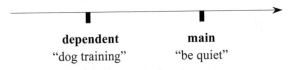

If the dependent-clause event takes place after or simultaneously with the main-clause event, the dependent clause is expressed with a non-past form.

警察で働く犬を訓練した。
"I trained dogs that would/will work for the police."

main   dependent
"training"   "working"

犬がほえているのが聞こえた。
"I heard a dog barking."

main/dependent
"hearing"/"barking"

Expressions of timing involving dependent clauses

In this section, we study various expressions of timing involving dependent clauses.

[V-plain past] 後で "after"

Regardless of the tense of the main clause, use a past-tense form in a dependent clause introduced by 後で. This is because 後で orders the main clause after the dependent clause on a timeline.

金魚鉢の水をかえた後で、金魚にえさをやる。
"After I change the water of the fish bowl, I will feed the goldfish."

金魚鉢の水をかえた後で、金魚にえさをやった。
"After I changed the water of the fish bowl, I fed the goldfish."

[V-plain non-past] 前に "before"

Conversely, use a non-past-tense form for a 前に-clause regardless of the tense of the main clause because 前に orders the main clause before the dependent clause on a timeline.

シャンプーをする前に、ブラッシングをする。
"I brush (my dog) before giving him a shampoo."

シャンプーをする前に、ブラッシングをした。
"I brushed (my dog) before giving him a shampoo."

There are many other expressions of timing that order the subordinate and the main clause on a timeline. We will study 間, うち, ところ, and ばかり next.

[V-plain non-past] 間 "while"

間, a noun literally meaning "space between," also has the extended meaning, "while." 間 introduces a dependent clause in such way that the main clause condition lasts simultaneously with the dependent clause condition. Therefore, use a non-past-tense form for an 間-clause regardless of the tense of the main clause.

あの犬は、飼い主が出かけている間ずっとないている。
"That dog barks for the entire time while his owner is out."

ねずみは、猫が起きている間は出て来なかった。
"The mouse did not come out as long as the cat was awake."

If the temporal particle に is not attached to the 間-clause, as in the above examples, both the 間-clause and main clause tend to describe a progressive or stative condition.

[V-plain non-past] 間に "while"

When に is attached to the 間-clause, the main clause must contain an eventive predicate. This is because に has the function of narrowing down the temporal frame to a point (*see BJ* Unit 5).

犬は、飼い主がいない間に塀の下に大きな穴を掘った。
"The dog dug a big hole under the fence while his owner was away."

猫は私がトイレに行っている間にテーブルの上の魚を食べた。
"My cat ate the fish on the table while I was in the bathroom."

[V-plain non-past] うちに "while"

うちに is similar to 間に, but its dependent clause condition lasts for a shorter time than that of 間に. Therefore, it often appears with an ADVERB such as ちょっと "a little," as in the following:

子猫はちょっと見ないうちにすっかり大きくなった。
"The kitten has grown quite a bit while I was away for a short period of time."

Also, うちに is preferred to 間に if the duration of the dependent clause condition is feared to be short.

犬が寝ているうちに犬小屋の前のボールをひろおう。
"Let's pick up the ball in front of the dog house while the dog is asleep."

[V-plain] ところ "the very moment"

ところ, whose basic spatial meaning is "place," has the extended meaning "the very moment." Its effect is a lively depiction of an on-going event as if one is broadcasting "play-by-play" or explaining images captured in film frames.

犬は、フリスビーを追いかけているところです。
"The dog is chasing after a Frisbee (right now)."

犬は、フリスビーをつかまえるところです。
"The dog is about to catch the Frisbee."

犬は、フリスビーを持って来たところです。
"The dog has just brought the Frisbee."

Notice that, by changing the form of the action verb before ところ you can describe an event as it is about to happen, is happening, or has just happened.

A ところ-clause is often used in inquiries into on-going activities.

今何(を)して(い)るところ?
"What are you doing?"

A ところ-clause also appears in various other grammatical contexts.

犬は、フリスビーを追いかけているところでした。
"The dog was chasing after a Frisbee (at that moment)."

犬がフリスビーをつかまえるところで、映画が終わりました。
"The movie ended at the scene where the dog was about to catch the Frisbee."

犬がフリスビーを持って来たところに、野球のボールが飛んで来ました。

"Just as the dog brought the Frisbee to me, a baseball came flying over."

― [V-plain past] ばかり "just now"

ばかり is somewhat similar to ところ. Combined with a past-tense form, it also depicts a moment when an event has just happened.

子猫は生まれたばかりだ。

"The kitten was just born."

The difference is that, deriving from its basic meaning "only," ばかり in this context means that the condition was barely brought about. Therefore, it implies either that the situation is too precarious or unstable to warrant any further action. In the case of the above sentence, the implication is that the kitten is still helpless. In the following sentence, the implication is that one should not feed the fish again soon.

さっき金魚にえさをやったばかりだ。

"I fed the goldfish just now."

If you do not want to add such an implication, use ところ. For instance, if you want to report breaking news with an assuring tone, use ところ rather than ばかり.

最新のニュースが入りました。今、パンダの赤ちゃんが生まれたところです。

"Latest breaking news has come in. A baby panda was just born."

Or if you want to emphasize that something has happened with good timing, use ところ, as in the following:

いいタイミング。パンダの赤ちゃんは、今起きたところ。

"Good timing. The panda cub has just woken up."

Converting this last sentence into one with ばかり would add the unintended implication that your visit to the zoo was not well timed.

パンダの赤ちゃんは、今起きたばかりです。

"The panda cub has just woken up (and not ready for public viewing)."

You can, of course, cancel such an implication with an additional sentence, as in the following:

パンダの赤ちゃんは、今起きたばかりですけど、ここから見られます。

"The panda cub has just woken up, but you can see her from here."

[V-stem] ながら "while"

Above we have studied expressions of timing involving dependent clauses. Among them were 間 and うち, often translated into "while." There is another expression of timing that is often translated into "while." This is ながら, which follows a STEM FORM and indicates a secondary simultaneous action.

名前を呼びながら、猫をさがした。

"I looked for my cat while calling her name."

The expressions 間 and うち connect independent events. Therefore, the subjects of the main and the dependent clauses do not have to be identical in sentences containing 間 or うち:

妹が家の中をさがしている間、私が庭をさがした。

"While my younger sister was searching the interior of the house, I searched the yard."

On the other hand, the subject of the main verb is the same as the subject in the ながら construction. Here are some more examples:

犬はお手をしながら、私の顔を見ました。

"The dog looked at me while giving me his paw."

ハミングバードは飛びながら、花の蜜を吸います。

"Hummingbirds drink nectar while flying."

Recall that in *BJ* Unit 6 we said that a て-FORM can describe the manner of an action in a sentence such as the following:

この教室ではボールを使って犬を訓練します。

"In this class, we train dogs using balls."

This sentence means that using balls is the primary means by which dog training is conducted. The ながら construction cannot be used in such a situation because it only denotes a simultaneous action rather than the manner in which the main action is carried out. The following sentence is anomalous for this reason.

× この教室ではボールを使いながら犬を訓練します。
"In this class, we train dogs while using balls."

On the other hand, the ながら construction is perfect for the following situation where the sense of purposefulness is absent from the highlighted action.

テレビを見ながら、宿題をした。
"I did my homework while watching TV."

In fact, the ながら construction is often used to criticize someone who cannot focus on one thing.

テレビを見ながら、宿題をしてはいけない。
"You may not do your homework while watching TV."

Exercise 4.1

Based on the following self-introduction, formulate verification questions in such a way that you indicate that you believe to have acquired each piece of information in a previous exchange.

私の名前は、杉田です。慶応大学の学生で、2年生です。
出身は、新潟です。専攻は、工学です。

Exercise 4.2

Choose the appropriate form for each sentence. You can check the meaning of each sentence in the Key to exercises.

1. スミスさんは、宿題の作文を{出す/出した}前にもう一度漢字を見直しました。

2. 私が{乗る/乗った}特急が、ホームに来ました。

3. {読む/読んだ}新聞は、この上にもどしてください。

4. 友だちが{来る/来た}までコーヒーショップで待ちました。

5. 誰かが歌を歌って{いる/いた}のが聞こえました。

6. 文句を{言う/言った}後で、自分の間違いに気がつきました。

Exercise 4.3

Fill in the blanks with the appropriate temporal expression. You can
check the meaning of each sentence in the Key to exercises.

1. 車は、信号が赤になる(　)に交差点に入りました。

2. 私は、運転し(　)ラジオを聞きます。

3. 私が運転している(　)友だちはずっととなりで寝ていました。

4. 私が寝ている(　)に車は山を越えました。

5. 子供が起きない(　)に早くプレゼントをかくしましょう。

Exercise 4.4

Change the verb in the parentheses into the appropriate form. You can
check the meaning of the passage in the Key to exercises.

Two travelers on the cell phone at an airport:

A: もしもし、どこにいるの?

B: 免税店。みどりはどこ?

A: さっきゲートに(着く)ところ。急いだ方がいいよ。ファースト
クラスの搭乗があと2、3分で(始まる)ところだから。

B: 大丈夫、心配しないで。今、レジで(待つ)ところだけ
ど、すぐ終わるから。

Exercise 4.5

Choose the more appropriate form. You can check the meaning of each sentence in the Key to exercises.

1. さっき食べた{ばかり/ところ}だから、まだ晩ご飯は食べられません。

2. 今、服を全部スーツケースに入れた{ばかり/ところ}で、一休みしてるの。

3. 買った{ばかり/ところ}の携帯電話が壊れた。

4. 最後に2人が再会した{ばかり/ところ}で、映画が終わった。

5. ゴルフは、まだ始めた{ばかり/ところ}だから、下手なんです。

Exercise 4.6

Complete the description of the pictures using ながら.

1. 土曜日の朝、川口さんは音楽を_____

2. 佐野さんは、テレビを_____

3. 谷さんは、コーヒーを_____

UNIT 5
Shifting perspectives

Main target grammar in this unit

日本語を話す vs. 日本語が話される、届けられる vs. 届く

A single event may be described in more than one way depending on one's perspective. For instance, the verbs "come" and "go" can describe an identical event from the opposite viewpoints. Grammatical constructions can also contribute to shifts in perspectives. For instance, the sentence "Mary encouraged John" and its passive counterpart "John was encouraged by Mary" describe roughly the same event but from two different perspectives. In this unit, we will study how Japanese grammar expresses this type of shifts in perspective as well as what motivates such shifts.

Active and passive sentences

Like English, Japanese has active and passive sentences. When someone does something to someone else, the event can be described in two ways. An active sentence describes it from the perspective of the AGENT, an active participant who initiates and carries out the action. The passive counterpart takes the perspective of the affected party that is on the receiving end of the action. Thus, the subject of the active sentence below is the agent, whereas the subject of the passive counterpart is the affected party.

Active

Agent = Subject	Affected = Direct object	V (Active form)
先生が	ケンを	しかった。
The teacher scolded Ken.		

Passive

Affected = Subject	Agent	V (Passive form)
ケンが	せんせい 先生に	しかられた。
Ken was scolded by the teacher.		

The direct object of the active sentence appears as the subject in the passive sentence. Similarly, below, the interactive target, which is marked by に in the active sentence, appears as the subject in the passive counterpart.

Active

Agent = Subject	Interactive target		V (Active form)
がいこくじん 外国人が	わたし 私に	にほんぶんか 日本文化について	き 聞きました。
A foreign national asked me about Japanese culture.			

Passive

Interactive target = Topic/Subject	Agent		V (Passive form)
わたし 私は	がいこくじん 外国人に	にほんぶんか 日本文化について	き 聞かれました。
I was asked by a foreign national about Japanese culture.			

In addition, the passive sentences contain special passive verb forms, which we will study below.

Passive forms

The formation of passive forms is quite regular. To formulate passive forms for **ONE-ROW VERBS**, drop る and attach られる.

た 食べる	→	た 食べられる	"be eaten"
いじめる	→	いじめられる	"be bullied"

43

To formulate passive forms of **FIVE-ROW VERBS**, replace the last *u*-row syllable with a corresponding *a*-row syllable and add れる, except that you should use わ for *u*-ending verbs. (*See* Appendix B for more examples.)

怒る → 怒られる "be scolded"
使う → 使われる "be used"

The passive counterparts of the two irregular verbs are as follows:

する → される "be done"
くる → こられる (*See* Unit 20 for the meaning of this form.)

The derived passive forms conjugate as one-row verbs regardless of the original verb type. The following table shows the **CONJUGATION** pattern of passive forms using おこられる "be scolded" as an example.

Plain conjugation of passive forms

	Affirmative	Negative
Non-past	おこられる "(will) be scolded"	おこられない "(will) not be scolded"
Past	おこられた "was scolded"	おこられなかった "was not scolded"

Expressing the non-subject agent

In passive sentences, the agent phrase does not appear as the が-marked subject. Instead, it appears with the **NON-SUBJECT AGENT PARTICLE** に "by" or the phrase によって "by means of." (The subject is either the affected party or the interactive target as we have already seen.)

ケンが先生にしかられた。
"Ken was reprimanded by the teacher."

東大寺は745年に聖武天皇によって建てられた。
"Todaiji was built in 745 by Emperor Shomu."

The difference between に and によって is that に is used when the agent is in a personal relationship with the non-agent subject, whereas によって is used when the agent is in an impersonal or formal relationship.

Such に-marked non-subject agents can also precede the non-agent subject phrase.

先生<ruby>せんせい</ruby>にケンがしかられた。
"Ken was reprimanded by the teacher."

聖武天皇<ruby>しょうむてんのう</ruby>によって東大寺<ruby>とうだいじ</ruby>は745年<ruby>ねん</ruby>に建<ruby>た</ruby>てられた。
"Todaiji Temple was built in 745 by Emperor Shomu."

The non-subject agent phrase may be omitted if it is understood from the context or is unknown or insignificant.

平安京<ruby>へいあんきょう</ruby>は、794年<ruby>ねん</ruby>に建<ruby>た</ruby>てられた。
"Heiankyo (the old capital of Japan) was built in 794."

Also a から-marked source phrase rather than a non-subject agent phrase may appear.

ワシントンの桜<ruby>さくら</ruby>は、1912年<ruby>ねん</ruby>に日本<ruby>にほん</ruby>から贈<ruby>おく</ruby>られました。
"The cherry trees in Washington, DC were given by Japan in 1912."

Using passive sentences

One major objective of using passive sentences is to **maintain DISCOURSE coherence**. For instance, of the two sentences below, the first one is more coherent and easier to follow. This is because the two parts of the sentence have the same subject, Ken, as a result of the second part being a passive sentence. By contrast, the second sentence is harder to follow because the subject switches from Ken to the teacher in the middle of a sentence.

o ケンはいたずらをして、先生<ruby>せんせい</ruby>にしかられた。
"Ken pulled a prank and was reprimanded by the teacher."
(*Subject*: Ken → Ken)

× ケンはいたずらをして、先生<ruby>せんせい</ruby>がケンをしかった。
"Ken pulled a prank, and the teacher reprimanded him."
(*Subject*: Ken → the teacher)

Another use of passive sentences is to suggest an **animate subject's lack of control** in a given event. For instance, the following passive sentence strongly implies that Mary had neither anticipated nor reciprocated John's action:

メアリーはジョンにキスされた。
"Mary was kissed by John."

Passive sentences also allow the focus to shift from a non-significant agent phrase to the focal object. This usage is most prevalent in journalistic reports or academic discussions.

スペイン語は南米でも話されている。
"Spanish is being spoken in South America, too."

あの俳優は広く知られている。
"That actor is widely known."

平安京は、794年に建てられた。
"Heiankyo was built in 794."

Note that merely dropping the subject in the active counterpart does not achieve the same result. The following sounds odd because the subject-agent tends to be understood as the speaker in the absence of some contextual cue indicating otherwise:

× 平安京は、794年に建てた。
"(I) built Heiankyo in 794."

CAUSATIVE SENTENCES, which we will study in depth in Unit 20, can also combine with the passive construction. For instance, instead of using the following causative sentence, in which the emperor is in the focus,

聖武天皇は、一流の大工たちに東大寺を建てさせた。
"Emperor Shomu ordered master carpenters to build Todaiji Temple."

you can use the following causative-passive sentence and bring the carpenters into focus:

一流の大工たちが東大寺を建てさせられた。
"Master carpenters were ordered to build Todaiji Temple."

(*See* Unit 20 for more details.)

Verbs incompatible with the passive construction

Some verbs do not appear in passive forms even if their approximate English counterparts do. For example, stative verbs such as 分かる "understand" and 要る "need" are excluded because they lack volitional agents. Use 理解する "comprehend" instead of 分かる.

× ブラック・ホールはまだよく分かられていない。
(*intended*: "Black Holes are not well understood yet.")

o ブラックホールはまだよく理解されていない。
"Black Holes are not well understood yet."

The verbs of giving あげる/くれる "give" (*see BJ* Unit 24) are paired specifically on the basis of a contrast in perspective. Therefore, no further shift in perspective via a grammatical construction is possible for either member.

× プレゼントがあげられた。
(*intended*: "A present was given.")

On the other hand, verbs that are not paired, such as 贈る "give" and 与える "give," are compatible with the passive construction.

o プレゼントが贈られた。
"A present was given."

Additionally, verbs that describe reciprocal actions, such as 会う "meet" and 結婚する "marry," cannot occur in the passive construction.

代表者が山田さんに会った。
"A representative met Mr. Yamada."

× 山田さんは代表者に会われた。
(*intended*: "Mr. Yamada was met by a representative.")

o 山田さんは代表者に出迎えられた。
"Mr. Yamada was met/greeted by the representative."

Passive forms versus intransitive verbs

In Unit 2, we saw that Japanese has many transitive-intransitive pairs such as 届ける "deliver" and 届く "be delivered." The intransitive member of such a pair is often translated into a passive form in English, as shown below:

花束が届いた。
"A bouquet arrived/was delivered."

The difference between this and the following sentence, which contains the passive form of the transitive verb 届ける, is obscured in translation.

花束が届けられた。
"A bouquet was delivered."

However, Japanese speakers sense a clear difference between the two sentences. This is because only the passive version indicates that the delivery involved someone's deliberate action. The intransitive version, which lacks this meaning of human agency, is the norm when describing electronic delivery.

友人からEメールが届いた。
"An email arrived from my friend."

Exercise 5.1

Following the example, produce the passive conjugations of the following verbs.

Example

見る "look"→
見られる　見られない　見られた　見られなかった

1. 置く "put" →

2. 忘れる "forget" →

3. ひらく "open (double doors)" →

4. 読む "read" →

5. 使う "use" →

6. 減らす "reduce" →

7. する "do" →

Exercise 5.2

Identify the subject of each sentence and translate the sentence.

1. ドラエモンは世界中の人々に親しまれている。
2. 今からちょうど100年前にこの家が建てられました。
3. ダウンロードしたファイルにウイルスが含まれていた。
4. あの人はどうして先生と呼ばれているんですか。
5. 各地でボランティア活動が行われている。
6. 今年は例年より多い積雪量が報告されている。

Exercise 5.3

Paying attention to the forms of the verbs, insert appropriate particles in parentheses. **Do not** use は or も. You can check the meaning of each sentence in the Key to exercises.

1. 私の母は高校で英語(　　)教えている。
2. タイの大学でも日本語(　　)教えられている。
3. 日本の酒(　　)世界中(　　)飲まれているんですか。
4. ローリングが新作を発表するの(　　)待たれている。
5. ホワイトハウス(　　)建てられたのは1800年だった。

Exercise 5.4

Choose the appropriate option. You can check the meaning of each sentence in the Key to exercises.

1. 今朝寝ていた時に、電話で{起こした/起こされた}から、眠い。
2. 朝食にトーストを焼いて、紅茶を{入れた/入れられた}。

3. 日本で最初の切手は1871年に{発行した/発行された}。

4. この本は今世界中の人が{読んでいる/読まれている}。

5. アメリカの大統領は、世界中の人々に{注目している/注目されている}。

6. グッゲンハイム美術館は、フランク・ロイド・ライトによって{設計した/設計された}。

7. 取引先の社長から開店祝いの花が{届けた/届けられた}。

8. 外国への小包には、昔は船が{使っていた/使われていた}が、今は、たいていの人が航空便を{使う/使われる}。

Exercise 5.5

Choose the appropriate option. You can check the meaning of each sentence in the Key to exercises.

1. 長引いていた風邪がやっと{治った/治された}。

2. 仕事場にいる主人からテキストメッセージが{届きました/届けられました}。

3. 昨晩玄関のインターフォンが{壊れた/壊された}。たぶん犯人は酔っ払いだろう。

4. 油汚れは{落ち/落とされ}にくいから、厄介だ。

5. 洗濯物が{乾いた/乾かされた}から、入れてくれない?

6. 弟は、無理矢理、ポニーに{乗って/乗せられて}泣いた。

7. 高速道路でのろのろ運転して、警官に{止まった/止められた}。

8. 私は両親を早くなくして、祖母に{育ちました/育てられました}。

UNIT 6
Gender

> **Main target grammar in this unit**
>
> Gender-specific vocabulary, sentence endings, and patterns

If invited to speak at a formal gathering such as a graduation or wedding ceremony, both Japanese men and women use polite and **HONORIFIC/ HUMBLE** expressions, minimizing the gender differences. However, in casual contexts, gender differences can be quite pronounced, to the extent that writers take advantage of the contrasts to signify who is speaking, without clearly identifying the speaker. For instance, if the following conversation is taking place at a couple's home, you are supposed to assume that speaker A is the husband and speaker B the wife, even though there is no explicit identification.

A: さあ、食べましょう。
"All right. Let's eat."

B: あれ、停電だ。いやだな。
"Oh, the light went out. What a nuisance!"

A: 大丈夫よ。すぐつくわよ。すわりなさいよ。
"We will be fine. The light will come back soon. Sit down."

B: ろうそくどっかにあっただろ。さがしてくれよ。
"I suppose we had candles somewhere. Will you look for them, please?"

In this unit, we will study some of the typical manners in which gender is marked in the Japanese language.

51

Vocabulary

Honorific and humble verb forms

Women tend to use honorific/humble vocabulary as well as honorific/
humble patterns such as [V-て] くださる, お [V-stem] になる, and [V-て] さ
しあげる (*see BJ* Unit 10) more frequently than men, even in informal
settings.

これ、お隣からいただいたの。[humble verb]
"I was given these by our neighbor."

見てくださる?
"Would you have a look at it?"

もうお帰りになったって。
"I was told that she has already left for home."

Men are likely to resort to these forms only in very formal settings where
polite endings are obligatory.

会長は、もうお帰りになったそうです。
"I heard that the CEO has already left for home."

Honorific prefixes

Both male and female speakers can use the honorific prefixes お and ご
for words relating to respected individuals or their possessions. The
choice between お and ご depends on individual words, but there is a
tendency for **SINO-JAPANESE** words to be marked with ご.

お大事に	"Please take care of yourself."
お宅	"your/his/her/their house"
お庭	"your/his/her/their garden"
ご両親	"your/his/her/their parents"

In addition, some common expressions usually contain an honorific prefix
and are used regularly by both men and women.

ご飯	"cooked rice"
お茶	"green tea"
お金	"money"
おみやげ	"souvenir"

Some combinations are used more frequently by women, but they may also be used by men without sounding effeminate.

おすし	"sushi"
お酒 _{さけ}	"alcoholic beverage"
おはし	"chopsticks"
お弁当 _{べんとう}	"lunch box"

Men can also use some combinations considered feminine to "sweeten" the speech addressed to a small child. (These forms do not have to refer to a child's possessions.)

お人形 _{にんぎょう}	"doll"
お花 _{はな}	"flower"
お魚 _{さかな}	"fish"
ご本 _{ほん}	"book"

Some other combinations are considered hyper-feminine or to be specific to the service industry.

お紅茶 _{こうちゃ}	"black tea"
お教室 _{きょうしつ}	"class (for a hobby)"
おコーヒー	"coffee"
おビール	"beer"

First- and second-person pronouns

Japanese has more than one first-person and one second-person pronoun. In formal contexts, both men and women can use 私 (or わたくし) to refer to themselves. However, in informal contexts, men are more likely to use 僕 or 俺, and women 私 or あたし. The difference between 僕 and 俺 is that 俺 is more "rough-and-tumble" and often functions as an expression of male camaraderie. Women's first-person pronouns are not associated with such a sense of camaraderie.

Certain second-person pronouns, such as 君 and お前, may only be used by male speakers. *See BJ* Unit 10 for more on the use of Japanese **PERSONAL PRONOUNS.**

Exclamatives

The second area where gender differences manifest themselves is that of the EXCLAMATIVES. A few exclamatives are considered exclusively feminine or masculine.

feminine: あら (noticing)
　　　　　　 まあ (surprise, sympathy)

masculine: おお (noticing, impressed)
　　　　　　 おい (attracting attention)
　　　　　　 よお ("tough-guy" greeting)
　　　　　　 やあ (friendly greeting)

These are used as shown in the following:

おい、あれ、見ろよ。 [male]
"Hey, look at that."

あら、虹だわ。まあ、きれい。 [female]
"Oh, it's a rainbow. Wow, it's beautiful."

Sentence endings

The third area where gender is differentiated is that of conversation and question particles. Conversation particles appear at the ends of sentences to express the speaker's attitude toward the listener. In addition to the basic ね and よ (*see BJ* Unit 5), さ, わ, ぜ, and ぞ are also used frequently in casual conversation. These conversation particles are differentiated by gender. Male and female speakers also use the question particles differently. In the following, we will look at them closely.

Emphatic particles

First, in casual contexts, some female speakers may add わ (with rising intonation) to a sentence in order to add mild emphasis.

Female only

分かったわ　　　　　　やさしいわ　　　　　　簡単だわ
"I got it."　　　　　　　"It's easy."　　　　　　"It's simple."

The particle よ can be added to these for reassurance.

分<ruby>わ</ruby>かったわよ   やさしいわよ   簡<ruby>かん</ruby>単<ruby>たん</ruby>だわよ
"I got it."   "It's easy."   "It's simple."

To seek agreement, ね is added.

分<ruby>わ</ruby>かったわ(よ)ね   やさしいわ(よ)ね   簡<ruby>かん</ruby>単<ruby>たん</ruby>だわ(よ)ね
"You got it, no?"   "It's easy, no?"   "It's simple, no?"

In standard Japanese, male speakers use ぜ, ぞ, and さ instead of わ for emphasis.

Male only

分<ruby>わ</ruby>かったぜ   やさしいぜ   簡<ruby>かん</ruby>単<ruby>たん</ruby>だぜ
"I got it!"   "It's easy!"   "It's simple!"

分<ruby>わ</ruby>かったぞ   やさしいぞ   簡<ruby>かん</ruby>単<ruby>たん</ruby>だぞ
"I got it!"   "It's easy!"   "It's simple!"

分<ruby>わ</ruby>かったさ   やさしいさ   簡<ruby>かん</ruby>単<ruby>たん</ruby>さ
"I got it, of course." "It's easy, of course." "It's simple, of course."

The particle さ is similar to "of course" or "no doubt." Unlike the particles わ, よ, ぞ, and ぜ, which emphasize one's conviction and therefore are compatible with the assertive, non-past COPULA form だ, the particle さ emphasizes the matter-of-fact nature of the situation and is incompatible with the ending だ (*see also* Unit 7).

Male speakers may use (よ)な to seek agreement. The combination よな is friendlier than な alone.

分<ruby>わ</ruby>かった(よ)な   やさしい(よ)な   簡<ruby>かん</ruby>単<ruby>たん</ruby>だ(よ)な
"You got it, no?"   "It's easy, no?"   "It's simple, no?"

Finally, よ attached directly to a predicate is gender-neutral.

分<ruby>わ</ruby>かったよ   やさしいよ   簡<ruby>かん</ruby>単<ruby>たん</ruby>だよ
"I got it."   "It's easy."   "It's simple."

Question particles

The question particle か is generally avoided in casual questions. The question intonation suffices. This is because a PLAIN form combined with か brings out the sense of confrontation or interrogation. However, precisely because of this possibility, a dominant male speaker may choose to use か in casual questions.

分かった**か**　　　やさしい**か**　　　簡単**か**
"Did you get it?"　"Is it easy?"　　　"Is it simple?"

When asking a junior person a question, men can use the softer question particle かい in order to sound less domineering.

分かった**かい**　　やさしい**かい**　　簡単**かい**
"Did you get it?"　"Is it easy?"　　　"Is it simple?"

A male speaker may also add か to a plain statement in order to convey that he has just made the realization.

分かった**か**　　　やさしい**か**　　　簡単**か**
"So they got it."　"So it's easy."　　"So it's simple."

Since an answer is not expected from the audience, such a quasi-question does not carry a confrontational tone. Nevertheless, female speakers avoid using か in this manner except in a few fixed expressions such as そうか "I see" and だめか "I see. It's no good."

Both male and female speakers can use the combination かな "I wonder."

分かった**かな**　　やさしい**かな**　　簡単**かな**
"Wonder if they　"Wonder if it's easy." "Wonder if it's simple."
got it."

In addition, women use かしら "I wonder."

分かった**かしら**　　やさしい**かしら**　　簡単**かしら**
"Wonder if they　"Wonder if it's easy." "Wonder if it's simple."
got it."

The particle か or かな added to a plain volitional form is also gender-neutral and non-confrontational.

行こう**か**。　　　　買おう**かな**。
"Shall we go?"　　　"I wonder if I should buy it."

だ and だろ(う)/でしょ(う)

The above differences stem from the traditional expectation that women's speech is less assertive. The particle わ is less assertive than ぞ, ぜ, or さ. The particle かしら is self-reflexive. For the same reason, the assertive ending だ is often deleted before よ or ね in women's speech, but in men's speech it must often be retained (*see also* Unit 7).

簡単**ね**　　　"It's simple, isn't it?" [female only]
簡単**よ**　　　"It's simple." [female only]

簡単**だね**　　"It's simple, isn't it?" [gender-neutral]
簡単**だよ**　　"It's simple." [gender-neutral]

Young male speakers may also use だい, a casual variant of だ in sentence-final position.

簡単**だい**! [male]
"It's simple!"

The particle だい may also appear in male speakers' **WH-QUESTIONS**.

何**だい**? [male]
"What is it?"

何がそんなにおかしいん**だい**? [male]
"What's so funny?"

Women are also expected to be more polite than men and to use the polite **ESTIMATION FORM** でしょ(う) rather than the plain estimation form だろ(う) (*see* Unit 15 and *BJ* Unit 20) in otherwise plain-style speech.

分かった**わ**よね。簡単**でしょ**? [female]
"You got it, didn't you? It's simple, isn't it?"

分^わかったよね。簡^{かんたん}単だろ? [male]
"You got it, didn't you? It's simple, isn't it?"

√Choice of imperatives

The choice of **IMPERATIVE FORMS** is another area where male and female speech contrast. Male speakers can use brusque command forms, which female speakers can use only in quotes. *See* Units 10 and 16 for details.

すわれよ	"Sit down."
食^たべろよ	"Eat."
言^いうなよ	"Don't tell that."

Female speakers tend to use the combination of a て-form and the conversation particle よ instead.

すわってよ	"Sit down."
食^たべてよ	"Eat."
言^いわないでよ	"Don't tell that."

√Male "tough-talk" patterns

To project a tough-guy image, some male speakers resort to "tough-talk" patterns. For instance, instead of using the pattern [V-て] いる (*see* Units 2 and 8), they use [V-て] やがる.

何^{なに}してやがるんだ?
"What the heck are you doing?"

Another characteristic feature of this type of speech is the change of adjectival endings [*a*- or *o*-row syllable + い] to [*e*-row syllable + え].

高^{たか}い	→	たけえ	"expensive"
面^{おもしろ}白い	→	おもしれえ	"interesting"

Changing gender roles

So far, we have looked at the way in which gender is represented in the Japanese language. However, among young people, the contrast between male and female speakers is less pronounced because, increasingly, both use gender-neutral forms. In addition, teenage female speakers may use traditionally male patterns with friends.

A: つまんねえの。
"It's boring."

B: 何言ってんのさ。しっかりしろよ。
"What are you talking about? Straighten up!"

(The **MORA** nasal ん in つまんねえ and いってん derives from ら and る respectively.)

Because of these changing social expectations, the stylized gender differences utilized by writers may no longer mirror the reality at home. The conversation given in the beginning of this unit may be recast by a contemporary couple in a more gender-neutral manner, as below, making it a challenge for a reader to ascertain the gender of each speaker:

A: さあ、食べよう。
"All right. Let's eat."

B: あれ、停電だ。いやだな。
"Oh, the light went out. What a nuisance!"

A: 大丈夫だよ。すぐつくよ。すわんなよ。
"We will be fine. The light will come back soon. Sit down."

B: ろうそくどっかにあっただろ。さがしてくれよ。[male]
"I suppose we had candles somewhere. Will you look for them, please?"

However, some patterns, such as command forms, are still quite masculine – as seen in the last line above.

Traditionally, most women at work spoke less assertively and more politely than their male colleagues. As women began to occupy positions of authority, such women have come to express their authority, not by adopting male speech patterns, but rather by speaking politely yet firmly or by speaking like a guardian in charge of youngsters (*see* Unit 10 for examples).

Exercise 6.1

Change the form of the following utterances according to the specification in the square brackets. You can check the meaning of each sentence in the Key to exercises.

1. これ、食べませんか。　　[honorific]

2. 必ず行きます。　　[humble]

3. お醤油、取ってくれる?　[polite]

4. お醤油、取ってくれる?　[plain honorific]

5. 明日は、雨でしょう。　　[plain]

6. さあ、行こう。　　[polite]

Exercise 6.2

Select the most appropriate exclamative from the box below. Use each one only once. In the Key to exercises, you can check the meaning of each sentence excluding the exclamative.

a. あら　b. まあ　c. おお　d. おい　e. よお　f. やあ

1. (　　), こら、そこで何してるんだ!

2. (　　), こんなところにキノコがあるわ。

3. (　　), そりゃ、なかなかおもしろいな。

4. (　　), そんなひどいことがあったんですか。

5. (　　), 山口君。久しぶりだね。

6. (　　), お前、元気にしてたか。

Exercise 6.3

Suppose that you come across the following exchanges between a female and a male speaker in a novel that you are reading. Assuming no hierarchical relationship between the two, decide for each exchange which is the female speaker and justify your decision.

1. A: 電話番号調べて下さる?

   "Will you please check the telephone number?"

   B: うん、いいよ。

   "Sure."

2. A: 帰りは誰が運転する?

   "Who will drive on the way back?"

   B: 僕がするよ。

   "I will."

3. A: そろそろ行くぞ。

   "It's about time to go."

   B: 切符持った?

   "Do you have tickets?"

4. A: 今何時ごろ?

   "About what time is it now?"

   B: 5時ごろでしょう。

   "It's about five."

5. A: 疲れただろう?休めよ。

   "I suppose you are tired. Have a break."

   B: ううん、大丈夫。

   "No, I am OK."

6. A: リモコンみつからないな。

   "I can't find the remote."

   B: あら、そう?テーブルの下にない?

   "Is that so? Can't you find it under the table?"

7. A: 今晩何にしようか。

   "What should we eat tonight?"

   B: 焼肉はどうかしら。

   "How about grilled meat?"

8. A: これ、おいしいわよ。

   "This is delicious."

   B: うん、うまい。

   "Yeah, it's good."

9. A: 早くしろよ。

   "Let's get going."

   B: ちょっと待ってよ。

   "Wait a while."

10. A: はし、もう1本いるよ。

    "I need one more chopstick."

    B: はい、どうぞ。お酒ちょっと飲む?

    "Here, please. Will you have a drink?"

Exercise 6.4

Reverse the gender stereotyping of 2B, 3A, 4B, and 5A in Exercise 6.3.

UNIT 7

The plain non-past form of the copula

Main target grammar in this unit

いい話だ{ぞ/と言う/そうだ/が/から/し}、いい話の{はずだ/ようだ}、いい話なのだ、いい話{らしい/かしら}

The copula です/だ is part of noun predicate and な-**ADJECTIVE** conjugations. As explained in *BJ* Unit 6, the conjugation of the copula goes as follows.

Conjugation patterns of the copula

	Affirmative	*Negative*
	PLAIN	
Non-past	だ "am/are/is"	じゃない "am/are/is not"
Past	だった "was/were"	じゃなかった "was/were not"
	POLITE	
Non-past	です "am/are/is" [polite]	じゃないです じゃありません "am/are/is not" [polite]
Past	でした "was/were" [polite]	じゃなかったです じゃありませんでした "was/were not" [polite]

Of these, the plain non-past form だ exhibits curious distributional properties not shared by the other forms. That is, it is sometimes obligatory but it is also often dropped or changed to な or の. In this unit we will summarize these distributional characteristics of だ.

Casual speech sentence-final positions

Obligatory and optional だ- dropping

The plain non-past form だ functions more as an assertion marker than just a plain non-past form of the copula. Therefore, it is dropped in casual questions.

First, だ is dropped before any question particle in casual speech.

1時{か/かい/かしら/かな}。
"It's one o'clock, right?"

Second, questions in casual speech may end with a bare noun phrase or a な-adjective.

今日の昼ごはんは何?
"What's for today's lunch?"

もう食べる時間?
"Is it already time to eat?"

どんな食べ物が好き?
"(I wonder) what type of food do you like?"

だ is also dropped before さ, which indicates a matter-of-fact situation requiring no convincing.

もちろん、すしさ。
"Of course it's sushi."

In addition, だ can be dropped in casual statements in general.

A: これ、お母さんの作ったお弁当。
   "This is the box lunch that my mother prepared."

B: わあ、きれい(だ)!
   "Wow, that's pretty!"

Above, speaker A drops だ to avoid sounding too assertive. Speaker B may also drop だ, but s/he can also opt to use だ because the remark is a compliment.

Also, if other sentence-final elements are present to mitigate its impression of over-assertiveness, だ can stay in friendly statements, as in the following:

A: 今日の昼ごはんは、お母さんの作ったお弁当なんだ。
"See, today's lunch is a box lunch my mother prepared."

B: 僕のは、お父さんが作ったお弁当だよ!
"Mine is a box lunch my father prepared!"

√No だ- dropping

Assertive sentence-final particles commonly used by men that are assertive require だ.

時間だぞ。
"It's time."

時間だぜ。
"It's time."

時間だな。
"It's time. Am I right?"

Sentence-medial positions

Obligatory だ- dropping

Because it is an assertion marker, だ cannot appear with estimation forms such as かもしれない "there is a chance that ..." and らしい "looks like" (*see* Unit 15), even though these generally require plain predicates.

父の出た高校は これ かもしれない。
"The high school my father graduated from may be this."

校長は 頑固 らしいです。
"The principal looks like he is unbending."

Throughout the book, the contexts where だ is obligatorily dropped will be marked as in [P-plain$^{(da\text{-}drop)}$] かもしれない.

(*See* Unit 16 for obligatory and optional dropping of だ in INDIRECT QUOTATION of questions.)

Replacement by の or な

Generally speaking, noun-modifying clauses (*see BJ* Units 4 and 10) end with plain forms. However, だ is replaced by の or な (depending on whether the preceding element is a noun or a な-adjective) because noun-modifying clauses are not assertive clauses.

√ 昼休みが 1時間の 小学校

"primary school where the lunch recess is one hour long"

√ 食堂が 新しくて きれいな 中学校

"middle school whose cafeteria is new and clean"

Likewise, in patterns used for expressing intention or planning (*see* Unit 12), だ is replaced by の (の is the norm here because the preceding element in this context is a verbal noun rather than a な-adjective).

来週の部活は全部 キャンセルの 予定です。

"We are planning to cancel all the club activities next week."

In Unit 15, we will study AUXILIARY ADJECTIVES of conjecture such as はずだ and ようだ. Some of these patterns involve noun-modifying clauses, in which だ is replaced by の after a noun and by な after a な-adjective.

√ いとこが通っている中学校はあの あたりの はずです。 [noun]

"The middle school to which my cousin is commuting should be around there."

√ 最近の高校の校舎はどれも きれいな ようです。 [な-adjective]

"High school buildings these days all seem to be attractive looking."

Throughout the book, the contexts where だ is replaced by either の or な (depending on the predicate type) will be marked as in [P-plain$^{(no/na)}$] はずだ.

Like noun-modifying clauses, nominalized clauses (*see BJ* Unit 11) generally end with plain forms. However, だ is replaced by な if flanked by a な-adjective and the **NOMINALIZER** こと.

この高校の校長が 頑固な ことは有名だ。

"The fact that this high school's principal is unbending is well known."

When flanked by a noun phrase and こと, だ is replaced by だという (*see BJ* Unit 11) or である.

校長が 外国人だという ことは知らなかった。

"I did not know the fact that the principal is a foreigner."

校長が 外国人である ことは知っている。

"I know the fact that the principal is a foreigner."

And in front of the nominalizer の, だ is turned into な regardless of whether the preceding element is a noun phrase or a な-adjective.

校長が 頑固な のを知らないで話しに行った。

"I went to talk to the principal without knowing that he is unbending."

Expressions that include the nominalizer の, such as のだ (*see BJ* Unit 11) and ので (*see BJ* Unit 23), as well as the **DISJUNCTIVE CONNECTIVE** のに (*see* Unit 19), also require な.

校長は アメリカ人な のですよ。

"I am saying that the principal is an American."

部活は 7時までな のでおなかがすく。

"Because the club activity is until 7, I get hungry."

夏休みな のに学校の掃除に行く。

"Although it is the summer vacation, we go to the school for cleaning."

The focus construction marked by のは (*see BJ* Unit 11) also requires な rather than だ.

√ 子供たちが静かなのは給食の時間だけだった。

"It was only during the school lunch time that the children were quiet."

√ 休みなのは子供たちだけで、先生はみんな働いていた。

"It was only the children that were on vacation, and the teachers were all working."

Throughout the book, the contexts where だ is always replaced by な will be marked as in [P-plain$^{(na)}$] のに.

No だ- dropping

We have seen that だ must remain before an assertive sentence-final particle in casual speech. Sentence-medial contexts that require だ are also assertive contexts. They include constructions for quotation (*see* Unit 16), hearsay (*see* Unit 16), contrast (*see BJ* Unit 5), and reasoning (*see* Unit 9 and *BJ* Unit 5).

√ 先生は宿題は簡単だと言ったけど、ちっとも簡単じゃない。

[indirect quote]

"My teacher said that the assignment would be easy, but it is not at all easy."

√ 担任の先生は大阪の出身だそうです。 [hearsay]

"I hear that the home-room teacher is from Osaka."

√ 宿題は簡単だが、試験はむずかしい。 [contrast]

"The homework assignments are easy, but the tests are difficult."

√ 先生は新米だから、子供の扱い方は下手です。 [reason]

"Because the teacher is inexperienced, he is poor at handling children."

√ 教室はきれいだし、最新のコンピューターはあるし、いいなあ。 [listing reasons]

"Their classrooms are sparkling clean. On top of that, they have the newest computers. So I envy them."

Summary

In this unit, we have seen that the assertive function of だ restricts its form and distribution. The following table summarizes this.

Form and distribution of だ

	Sentence-final position in casual speech	Sentence-medial position
Dropped	in questions	before かもしれない, らしい
Changed to の or な	—	before a noun and the nominalizer こと
Changed to な	—	before the nominalizer の
Replacement by だという or である	—	between a noun and the nominalizer こと
Retained	before ぞ, ぜ, な	before と, そうだ, が, から, し

Exercise 7.1

Provide the plain-style counterpart of the following forms.

1. 楽しいです "it is enjoyable'
2. 晴れです "it is sunny"
3. 元気です "they are healthy"
4. インタビューです "it is an interview"
5. 美しいです "it is beautiful"
6. きれいです "it is clean/beautiful"

Exercise 7.2

Change the following utterances to the polite style.

1. どこ? "Where?"

2. 何^{なん}だった? "What was that?"

3. あの人^{ひと}、先生^{せんせい}なの? "Is she a teacher?"

4. 空気^{くうき}がとっても爽^{さわ}やか。 "The air is really refreshing."

5. そろそろ行^いく時間^{じかん}だよ。 "It's about time to go."

6. アイスクリーム好^すき? "Do you like ice cream?"

Exercise 7.3

Choose between な and の. You can check the meaning of each sentence in the Key to exercises.

1. アパートは駅前^{えきまえ}でとても便利^{べんり}{な/の}ようです。
   (*See also* Unit 15.)

2. 1階^{いっかい}が食料品^{しょくりょうひん}のスーパー{な/の}アパートに住^すんでいます。

3. 来週^{らいしゅう}の火曜日^{かようび}から3日^{みっか}関西^{かんさい}に旅行^{りょこう}{な/の}予定^{よてい}です。
   (*See also* Unit 12.)

4. 明日^{あした}は休^{やす}み{な/の}んですよ。

5. そのあたりのホテルは、1泊2万円^{いっぱくにまんえん}ぐらい{な/の}はずです。
   (*See also* Unit 15.)

6. 一番問題^{いちばんもんだい}{な/の}のは、誰^{だれ}も何^{なに}も言^いわなかったことです。

Exercise 7.4

Fill in the blanks with だ if necessary. Insert Ø if だ is not acceptable. You can check the meaning of each sentence in the Key to exercises.

1. このコップきれい(　　)かな?

2. これは、問題^{もんだい}(　　)ぞ。

3. ワシントンでも今週は大雪(　　)そうです。
   (*See also* Unit 16.)

4. 簡単(　　)から、子供でも使えます。

5. 週末は大雨(　　)らしいです。(*See also* Unit 15.)

6. 寝る時間(　　)からテレビは消しますよ。

Exercise 7.5

Choose between だ, な, の, and Ø. You can check the meaning of each
sentence in the Key to exercises.

1. 今晩は月がとてもきれい{だ/な/の/Ø}ようです。
   (*See also* Unit 15.)

2. 彼は、もちろん大学院生{だ/な/の/Ø}さ。

3. ここは、静か{だ/な/の/Ø}し、夜は星がよく見えます。
   (*See also* Unit 9.)

4. 建物の外はきたないけど、中はきれい{だ/な/の/Ø}かもしれな
   い。(*See also* Unit 15.)

5. お母さんがデザイナー{だ/な/の/Ø}友だちからスカーフをもら
   いました。

6. １２月{だ/な/の/Ø}のにとても暖かいです。
   (*See also* Unit 19.)

Part 2
Grammar by tasks

UNIT 8

Describing states

As we saw in *BJ* Unit 5, い-adjectives, な-adjectives, noun predicates, and stative verbs generally describe stable conditions and are identified as stative predicates (*see also* Unit 2 in this book). In addition, Japanese has various complex patterns for describing stable or sustained conditions. Some concepts will be familiar to English speakers, but others involve novel concepts and will be intriguing. In this unit, we will begin with the simplest of these patterns and gradually proceed to the more intriguing ones.

The progressive use of [V-て] いる

When the て-form of an action verb (*see* Unit 2) is combined with the verb いる "be, exist," the resulting pattern has the meaning of progressive action, either current or in the past.

今、地図を調べています。　　　　　　[present progressive]
"I am checking a map."

さっきガイドブックを読んでいました。 [past progressive]
"I was reading a travel book a while ago."

In *BJ* Unit 13, we saw that the verb いる is only used with animate subjects. However, in this auxiliary use, it is not limited to animate subjects.

75

客が電話をかけている。　　　　　　[animate subject]
"The guest is making a phone call."

部屋で電話が鳴っている。　　　　　[inanimate subject]
"The phone is ringing in the room."

In casual speech, ている is shortened to てる, and its negative counterpart to てない.

√ さっき電話が鳴ってたけど、もう鳴ってない。
"The phone was ringing a moment ago, but no more."

Action verbs combine with the [V-て] いる construction to mean "do something and stay in that condition" literally. The duration described with this pattern can be much longer than that described by the English progressive construction.

√ この2年間、世界中を旅行しています。仕事はしていません。
"I have been traveling all over the world for the past two years.
I have not been working."

Do not use this pattern in the sense of "planning for the future" as shown in the English progressive construction below:

I am going to Kyoto tomorrow. I am visiting many temples.

The Japanese [V-て] いる construction does not have this usage. To describe a plan, just use a non-past form (see also Unit 4).

√ 明日、お寺を見ます。(×見ています) [future]
"I am visiting temples tomorrow."

The resultant continuative use of [V-て] いる

Action verbs such as 見る "see" and 食べる "eat" describe actions that can potentially be continued without reaching a definite goal. In contrast, change-of-state verbs (see Unit 2 and BJ Unit 3) such as 結婚する "get married" and change-of-location verbs (see Unit 2) such as 着く "arrive" focus on the end point rather than the process.

夕方、ホテルのチャペルで結婚した。
"In the evening, we got married at the chapel of the hotel."

√ 昼ごろ、ホテルに着いた。
"We arrived at the hotel around noon."

When the auxiliary いる is combined with the て-form of such verbs, the combination means that a resultant state is or was maintained (i.e. resultant continuative).

√ もうホテルに着いていますか。
"Have they already arrived at the hotel?" [resultant cont. present]
(= Are they already at the hotel?)

√ お客さんはまだ来ていなかった。 [resultant cont. past]
"The guests had not come yet."
(= The guests were not here yet.)

Pay close attention to the following sentences. The first sentence does not mean that a wedding ceremony is going on; the couple is already married. The second sentence does not mean that the couple is on the way to a destination; they are already there.

その若いカップルは結婚している。
"The young couple is married."

その若いカップルはフランスに行っている。
"The young couple is in France."

Incidentally, this last sentence indicates that the couple originated elsewhere and is visiting France on a temporary basis. The following sentence, which lacks 行って, does not have that meaning:

その若いカップルは、フランスにいる。 [state]
"The young couple is in France."

When a change-of-state/location verb has a volitional subject and describes a change that takes place over a span of time rather than an instantaneous change, the action-in-progress reading is also available. The following sentence is thus ambiguous:

花嫁が教会に入っています。　　　[change-of-location verb]
"The bride is inside the church."
"The bride is entering the church now."

The [V-て] ある construction

There is another type of construction that means that a resultant condition is lasting. The [V-て] ある construction indicates that, as a result of an intentional action, something becomes ready. An overwhelming majority of the verbs that appear in this construction are transitive action verbs.

海側の部屋を予約してあります。
"We have made a reservation for an ocean-side room."

荷物を部屋に運んであります。
"We have carried the luggage to the room."

ベッドの上に毛布を出してあります。
"We have put out a blanket (from the closet) on the bed."

タオルをかけてあります。
"We have hung towels."

This construction, unlike the English construction "have done," is restricted to cases where the described condition sets the stage for the next step. For instance, the following sentence can be used only before, not after, you leave the hotel:

ホテル代は、払ってあります。
"I have (already) paid the hotel charge."
(We can check in/out without showing the credit card.)

The construction, like the [V-stem] たい-form (see BJ Unit 15), creates a combined stative predicate. The direct object of the transitive verb (see Unit 2 and BJ Unit 5) can be marked by が rather than を in this construction.

海側の部屋が予約してあります。
"An ocean-side room has been reserved."

荷物が部屋に運んであります。
"The luggage has been carried to the room."

ベッドの上に毛布が出してあります。
"A blanket (from the closet) has been put out on the bed."

√タオルがかけてあります。
"Towels have been hung."

As the English translations show, there is a slight difference between the pattern with を and the pattern with が. In the first type, the person's foresightedness is emphasized. The second type focuses on the readiness of the object. The person who did the action is hidden.

Transitive and intransitive verb pairs

As explained in Unit 2, Japanese has a large number of transitive-intransitive pairs, such as あける "open (something)" and あく "(something) opens." Verbs that come in transitive-intransitive pairs have specific semantic properties. That is, all transitive members of paired verbs are action verbs, whereas all intransitive members of paired verbs are change-of-state or change-of-location verbs. As a result, transitive members in the [V-て] いる construction receive an action-in-progress reading, whereas intransitive members in the [V-て] いる construction usually receive a resultant state reading. Furthermore, only transitive members appear in the [V-て] ある construction. In what follows, we will look at examples of each pattern.

Transitive members in [V-て] いる

When the て-form of a transitive member is followed by いる, the construction usually has a progressive meaning.

√窓を開けている。	"I am opening the window."
窓を閉めている。	"I am closing the window."
√電気をつけている。	"I am turning on the light."
√電気を消している。	"I am turning off the light."
√荷物を届けている。	"I am delivering luggage."

These sentences mean that the agents deliberately take time to complete the action.

Transitive members in [V-て] ある

The transitive members are also compatible with the [V-て] ある construction, which adds the meaning of foresightedness or readiness.

√ 天気がいいから、窓を開けてあります。

"Because the weather is good, the windows have been (intentionally) kept open."

√ すぐ前に隣のビルの窓が見えますから、カーテンを閉めてあります。

"Because the windows of the neighboring building are right in front, the curtains are kept drawn (intentionally)."

√ プール側のドアは、中から鍵がかけてあるから、外から入れません。

"The pool-side door is locked from inside (intentionally), so you cannot come in through it from outside."

Again, the direct object of the transitive verb can be marked by either が or を. The pattern with を focuses on the person's foresightedness, whereas the pattern with が focuses on the readiness of the object.

Intransitive members in [V-て] いる

When an intransitive member is used with いる, the construction usually gets the resultant continuative interpretation, which we saw in association with end-point focused verbs, such as 結婚する "get married."

√ 窓が開いている。   "The window is open."
√ 窓が閉まっている。   "The window is closed."
√ 電気がついている。   "The light is on."
√ 電気が消えている。   "The light is off."
√ 荷物が届いている。   "The luggage is here."

This is because the subjects of these intransitive verbs are usually inanimate and cannot deliberately take time to undergo the change. The focus therefore shifts to the resultant condition rather than the process. Observe additional examples:

海側のカーテンは閉まっていましたが、窓が開いていました。
"The curtains on the ocean side were closed, but the windows were open."

√タオルがぬれています。取り替えてください。
"The towels are wet. Please change them."

Unlike transitive members in [V-て] ある, intransitive members in [V-て] いる are used when the condition is unintentional or beyond the speaker's control.

あれ、鍵がかかっている。
"Oh, the door is locked."

外出から帰って来たら、ドアが開いていて、テレビがついていました。
"When I came back from my outing, I found the door open and the TV on."

√タオルは、もう乾いている?
"Is the towel dry now?"

Use this pattern to complain if you find your hotel room less than satisfactory. Even if you want to blame the management for negligence, you do not want to accuse them of malicious intent by using a transitive verb in [V-て] ある!

洗面台がよごれています。(×よごしてある)
"The wash basin is dirty."

√電球が切れています。(×切ってある)
"The bulb is burned out."

Summary

The following table summarizes the four patterns.

Patterns with [V-て] いる and [V-て] ある

を + transitive member + ている	Deliberate sustained action	ドアを開けている。 "I am opening the door." 鍵をかけている。 "I am locking it."
を + transitive member + てある	Foresightful action/ *iNtention*	ドアを開けてある。 "I have opened the door." 鍵をかけてある。 "I have locked it."
が + transitive member + てある	Readiness of an object	ドアが開けてある。 "The door is open for a reason." 鍵がかけてある "It has been locked."
が + intransitive member + ている	Condition not under control	ドアが開いている。 "The door is open." 鍵がかかっている。 "It is locked."

Exercise 8.1

Complete the following sentences using the [V-て] いる construction and the verbs given in parentheses.

1. 伊藤さんは、洗面所で顔を＿＿＿＿＿＿。(洗う)

   "Mr. Ito is washing his face in the bathroom."

2. 伊藤さんは、洗面所で歯を＿＿＿＿＿＿。(みがく)

   "Mr. Ito is brushing his teeth in the bathroom."

3. 伊藤さんは、ソファーの上で＿＿＿＿＿＿。（寝る）

   "Mr. Ito is sleeping on the sofa."

4. 伊藤さんは、窓のそばで新聞を＿＿＿＿＿＿。（読む）

   "Mr. Ito is reading the newspaper near the window."

5. 伊藤さんは、窓の外を＿＿＿＿＿＿。（見る）

   "Mr. Ito is looking at the outside."

Exercise 8.2

Match the English sentences 1–4 with the Japanese sentences a–d. The supplemental information in the parentheses is not included in a–d.

1. Ichiro and Midori were not married two years ago (when I last met them at a restaurant).
2. Ichiro and Midori got married two years ago.
3. Ichiro and Midori didn't get married two years ago.
4. Ichiro and Midori were married two years ago (when I last met them at a restaurant).

a. 一郎とみどりは、二年前結婚した。
b. 一郎とみどりは、二年前結婚していた。
c. 一郎とみどりは、二年前結婚していなかった。
d. 一郎とみどりは、二年前結婚しなかった。

Exercise 8.3

You are going on a trip with your friend. The following is your to-do list before the trip. You have checked off the tasks you have completed. Answer your friend's questions following the example. You can check the meaning of each dialog in the Key to exercises.

☑ 航空券を買う　　　　　□ 地図を調べる

☑ レンタカーを予約する　☑ ガイドブックを読む

□ ショーのチケットを取る　□ パッキングする

Example

> A: ホテルの予約した?
> "Have you made a reservation for a hotel?"

> B: うん、してある。/ううん、まだしてない。
> "Yes, I have. /No, I haven't."

1. 航空券、買った?
2. レンタカー、予約した?
3. ショーのチケット、取った?
4. 地図を調べた?
5. ガイドブックを読んだ?
6. パッキングした?

Exercise 8.4

Choose the appropriate verb for each sentence. You can check the meaning of each sentence in the Key to exercises.

1. 寝る前に電気を{消した/消えた}。
2. 風でろうそくが{消した/消えた}。
3. タオルを{ぬれて/ぬらして}顔をふいた。
4. コンピューターが{壊した/壊れた}。
5. 窓を{閉まって/閉めて}下さい。
6. コンピューターを{直して/直って}います。

Exercise 8.5

Choose the appropriate expression and translate the sentence.

1. おかしい。窓が{開いている/開けている}。
2. 鍵が{かけている/かかっている}から開けられません。

3. カーテンは、{閉めてあります/閉めています/閉まっています}。開けないでください。

4. よく見えません。電気を{ついて/つけて}ください。

5. タオルはちょっと待って下さい。今{かわいています/かわかしてあります/かわかしています}。

UNIT 9

Listing things and events

Main target grammar in this unit

友だちとか家族、話したり笑ったりする、大声で話すしよく笑うし

Japanese has grammatical patterns for listing things and events exhaustively or non-exhaustively. In this unit, we will study these patterns.

Exhaustive and non-exhaustive listing of things

Asked what local specialties you would like to eat, you can answer using one of the following patterns:

焼きそばとお好み焼きを食べたいです。
"I want to eat *yakisoba* (fried noodles) and *okonomiyaki* (Japanese-style pancake)."

焼きそばとかお好み焼きが好きです。
"I like *yakisoba* and *okonomiyaki*, for instance."

焼きそばやお好み焼きが好きです。
"I enjoy food like *yakisoba* and *okonomiyaki*."

The use of the particle と as in the first sentence implies that the list is exhaustive and that the speaker has named every item relevant for the time being. In contrast, とか in the second sentence, deriving from the particle と and the question particle か, means that the list is non-exhaustive; it is used to give representative samples. The particle や in the third sentence is similar to とか, but it is slightly less colloquial. (*See also BJ* Unit 5.)

Exhaustive listing of events: て-form

As you learned in *BJ* Unit 6, among other things a て-form connects a sequence of events.

大阪へ行って、天神祭を見ました。 [sequence of events]
"I went to Osaka and saw Tenjin Matsuri festival."

て-forms used in this manner imply that the events are ordered chronologically and exhaustively. That is, it is implied that the speaker has listed all and every relevant event as they occurred.

Non-exhaustive listing of events: [V-plain past] り、 [V-plain past] り、する

If you want to name just a few representative events that have happened without reference to their chronological order, use [V-plain past] り、 [V-plain past] り、する. The verb する at the end of the sentence carries the tense, aspect, and politeness information.

Non-exhaustive listing of events

Agent = Topic		Event 1 (V-plain past)	Event 2 (V-plain past)	V
私は	お祭りで	花火を見たり	かき氷を食べたり	しました。
At the festival, I did such things as watching fireworks and eating shaved ice.				

Giving two たり phrases as examples is very common, but any number of たり phrases can be given as examples.

お祭りで、たこ焼きを食べたりしました。
"At the festival, I did such things as eating *takoyaki*."

お祭りで、かき氷を食べたり、金魚すくいをしたり、花火を見たりしました。
"At the festival, I ate shaved ice, scooped goldfish, watched fireworks, and so on."

The たり form can also connect paired predicates such as "go/come" and "turn on/turn off." In such cases, the non-exhaustive meaning of the たり forms forces an iterative interpretation. That is, the two listed events are interpreted as alternating without an obvious end.

船が行ったり来たりしています。
"The boats are repeatedly going and coming."

明かりがついたり消えたりしていました。
"The lights were flickering on and off."

The する part may be dropped if the final predicate of the sentence summarizes the situation as a whole.

花火を見たり、かき氷を食べたり(して)楽しかったです。
"I had fun doing things like ~~goldfish scooping~~ and eating shaved ice." *fireworks—viewing*

The non-exhaustive patterns may also be used to "soften the edge" in colloquial speech. For instance, even if you have bought only one item, you can still use とか, as shown in the following:

お祭りで、たこ焼きとか食べたんだ。
"At the festival, I ate *takoyaki* and the like."

Similarly, you can use the たり pattern even if you have done only one thing.

お祭りで、たこ焼き食べたりしたんだ。
"At the festival, I did things like eating *takoyaki*."

Listing multiple reasons: [P-plain] し、 [P-plain] し、

Using the following pattern, you can list multiple reasons to support your proposal or statement. し usually attaches to a plain form except in extra polite speech.

Listing reasons

Reason 1 (P-plain)		Reason 2 (P-plain)		Main proposal/ statement
天気(てんき)もいい	し、	あまり暑(あつ)くない	し、	花火(はなび)を見(み)に行(い)きませんか。

The weather is nice, and (moreover) it's not too hot, so how about going to see fireworks?

√ 星(ほし)もよく見(み)えるし、川(かわ)からの風(かぜ)も涼(すず)しいし、ここは気持(きも)ちがいいねえ。

"We can see the stars clearly. Besides, the wind from the river is cool. So this place is pleasant, isn't it?"

√ 花火(はなび)はきれいだし、友(とも)だちには会(あ)えたし、お祭(まつ)りに来(き)てよかった。

"The fireworks are beautiful. Besides, I was able to see my friend. So it was good that I have come to the festival."

However, when the entire utterance is in the polite style, you can also use polite forms to increase the level of politeness.

美味(おい)しいものも食(た)べましたし、花火(はなび)も見(み)ましたし、本当(ほんとう)にいい日でした。

"We ate delicious food, saw the fireworks … it was a really wonderful day."

As in the case of たり, any number of し is possible, all incrementally strengthening the case, but it is most common to use one or two. Providing just one し-clause implies that there are other reasons.

もう遅(おそ)いし、そろそろ帰(かえ)りましょうか。

"It's getting late (among other reasons), so shall we go home now?"

The part that follows し is often left unsaid when the speaker is producing (an) excuse(s).

A: お祭(まつ)りに行(い)きませんか。

"Why don't we go to a festival?"

B: うーん、人ごみが多いし、ちょっと風邪気味だし…。

"Well, I don't like crowded places, and I have a little bit of a cold, so …"

The last し can also be replaced by a more logical marker for reason.

星もよく見えるし、川からの風も涼しいから、ここは気持ちがいいです。

"We can see the stars clearly. Moreover, the wind from the river is cool. Therefore, this place is pleasant."

Exercise 9.1

In the box below, Mr. Takahashi's likes and dislikes about animals are marked as follows: he likes it (♂), he does not like it (♀). Based on this information, decide whether each sentence is accurate.

ヘビ	"snake" (♀)	カエル	"frog" (♀)
トカゲ	"lizard" (♀)	ネコ	"cat" (♂)

(Animal species names are often written in *katakana*.)

1. [True / False]　　ネコが好きです。
2. [True / False]　　ヘビとトカゲとカエルが嫌いです。
3. [True / False]　　トカゲとかカエルが嫌いです。
4. [True / False]　　ネコやカエルが好きです。

Exercise 9.2

Answer the question concerning Ms. Suzuki's likes/dislikes about vegetables. Her likes and dislikes are marked in the same way as in Exercise 9.1.

たまねぎ	"onion" (♀)	ねぎ	"green onion" (♀)
にら	"garlic chive" (♀)	にんにく	"garlic" (♀)
トマト	"tomato" (♂)	ピーマン	"green pepper" (♂)

1. 鈴木さんは、どの野菜が嫌いですか。

2. 鈴木さんは、どんな野菜が嫌いですか。

Exercise 9.3

Provide the たり-forms of the following verbs.

1. 頼む   "request"
2. 誘う   "invite"
3. 調べる   "check"
4. 泣く   "cry"
5. 立つ   "stand"
6. 壊す   "destroy"
7. 飛ぶ   "fly"
8. 泳ぐ   "swim"
9. 掃除する "clean"
10. 来る   "come"

Exercise 9.4

Explain what type of activity Mr. Matsumoto does or likes/dislikes by naming representative samples. His likes and dislikes are marked in the same way as in Exercise 9.1.

doing laundry (♀)	skiing (♂)
cleaning the house (♀)	outdoor skating (♂)
doing dishes (♀)	ice hockey (♂)
cooking (♂)	
going to a restaurant with friends (♂)	
going to a movie with friends (♂)	
going to a party with friends (♂)	

1. 松本さんは、家事の中で、どんなことをするのが嫌いですか。
2. 松本さんは、冬にどんなスポーツをするのが好きですか。
3. 松本さんは、どんなことを友だちといっしょにするのが好きですか。

Exercise 9.5

Fill in the blanks with the appropriate expression. You can check the meaning of each sentence in the Key to exercises.

1. 駅前の大通りはクリスマスツリーの赤や緑のライトがついたり(　　　)して、とてもきれいです。

2. この冬の天気は変です。急に暖かく(　　　)寒く(　　　)します。

3. 山の上は寒くて、雨が(　　　)霧が出たりしました。

4. 人と話すのは好きじゃないので、パーティでは、ただ(　　　)食べたりします。

5. 宮本さんは、仕事でよく日本とニュージーランドを行ったり(　　　)します。

Exercise 9.6

Fill in the blanks with the reasons given in the parentheses. You can check the meaning of each sentence in the Key to exercises.

1. 今日は、＿＿＿＿＿＿＿＿＿＿(windy; cold)し、どこにも行かないで家にいます。

2. ＿＿＿＿＿＿＿＿＿＿(headache; fever)から、学校は休みます。

3. ＿＿＿＿＿＿＿＿＿＿(I like Japanese movies; Japanese culture is interesting)から、日本語を専攻します。

4. ＿＿＿＿＿＿＿＿＿＿(It's late; We have an early morning tomorrow)し、もう失礼しましょう。

UNIT 10

Demanding actions

Main target grammar in this unit

話せ、話すな、話してくれ、話せと言われた、話しなさい

In English, you can use imperative forms not only to give orders but also to give advice or to make a request.

Attention! **Stand** up.

Wear a hat to prevent sunburn.

Please **have** a seat. Someone will be with you shortly.

Japanese command forms carry more authoritarian tones than English imperative forms, but with appropriate adjustments they too can be used not only to give orders but also to gently nudge people to do something. In this unit, we will study the forms and nuances of various command forms in Japanese.

Brusque commands

Japanese bare imperative forms are considered extremely brusque and masculine (*see* Unit 6 for other masculine expressions). They are used regularly where strict chains of command exist, such as law enforcement or military organizations and university sport clubs. In such organizations, superior officers, coaches, upper class men, and the like may use bare imperative forms to give their subordinates orders. In addition, angry male customers may use these forms to confront store clerks.

Affirmative imperative forms of five-row verbs are created by substituting the last syllable of the plain non-past affirmative form with a corresponding *e*-row syllable.

Five-row verbs

言う	→	言え	"Say (it)!"
書く	→	書け	"Write!"
泳ぐ	→	泳げ	"Swim!"
話す	→	話せ	"Talk!"
待つ	→	待て	"Wait!"
死ぬ	→	死ね	"Die!"
飲む	→	飲め	"Drink!"
√帰る	→	帰れ	"Go home!"

For one-row verbs, add ろ to the base.

One-row verbs

√食べる	→	食べろ	"Eat!"
√見る	→	見ろ	"Look!"

There is a single exception to this pattern: the imperative form of the one-row verb くれる "give (to me)" is くれ "Give (it to me)!" not the expected くれろ.

くれる	→	くれ	"Give (it to me)!"

The imperative forms of the irregular verbs する "do" and 来る "come" are しろ and 来い, respectively.

Irregular verbs

する	→	しろ	"Do (it)!"
来る	→	来い	"Come!"

Below are some examples of how to use imperative forms:

こっちへ来い。	"Come here!"
√しっかり話を聞け。	"Listen carefully."

あっちへ行け。 "Go away!"

さっさと食べろ。 "Eat fast."

金、返せ。 "Give me the money back."

To issue a negative command, attach the negative particle な to the plain non-past affirmative form of a verb regardless of its conjugation type.

止まるな。 "Don't stop."

そんなこと言うな。 "Don't say that."

√こら、笑うな。 "Hey, don't laugh."

In addition to the "tough-guy" situations explained above, bare imperative forms are used, for example, for traffic signs such as the following because of the strong impact their brusqueness can deliver:

止まれ "Stop!"

スピード落とせ "Reduce the speed!"

√飲んだら乗るな "Don't drive if you've had a drink!"

Friendly demands

For imperative forms to be used in more ordinary conversation, an appropriate adjustment needs to be made to their ending. For instance, when male office workers go out to drink together, they may want to nudge each other to do something. They can do so by adding the conversation particle よ to a bare imperative form as in the following:

もっと飲めよ。 "Drink more."

ほんとのこと言えよ。 "Tell me the truth."

たまにはおごれよ。 "Pay for me sometimes."

笑うなよ。 "Don't laugh."

そんなこと言うなよ。 "Don't say that."

These expressions are not so brusque and can be directed to friends or younger acquaintances by male speakers.

くれ used as an **AUXILIARY VERB** after a て-form also creates acceptable forms for requesting actions.

自分でやってくれ。 "Please do it on your own."

これを見てくれ。 "Please have a look at this."

These expressions can be used by male bosses to give orders to their subordinates.

君が行ってくれ。
"You go, please."

先にあいさつしてくれ。
"Please welcome them first."

簡単に説明してくれ。
"Please explain it briefly."

よく調べてくれ。
"Please check it carefully."

報告書を書いてくれ。
"Please write a report."

The following examples contain a negative て-form:

まだ行かないでくれ。
"Please do not go yet."

このことは当面書かないでくれ。
"Please do not write about this for the moment."

Quoting commands

Bare command forms and command forms with the auxiliary くれ are used almost exclusively by men. However, it is not the case that female speakers never use these forms. This is because both male and female speakers can quote commands in verbatim fashion. Furthermore, both male and female speakers freely use command forms to quote brusque requests indirectly (*see also* Unit 16).

√ 部長は来週までに報告を**まとめろ**とおっしゃいました。
"The division chief told me to complete the report by next week."

√ 8時までに**来い**と言われたんだ。
"I was told to come by 8."

√ 携帯電話は**使うな**と怒られました。
"I was scolded that I should not use a cell phone."

The expressions 〜と言われました and 〜と怒られました are the passive versions of the quotation patterns 〜と言いました "said that" and 〜と怒りました "scolded that." (*See* Unit 16 for quotations and Unit 5 for passives.)

In the following example, the くれ version is used to reflect the solicitous tone of the main verb 頼まれました "was requested to":

代わりに会議に**出席してくれ**と頼まれました。
"I was asked to attend the meeting in his place."

Guardians' commands: [V-stem] なさい

So far, we have focused on male use of command forms. How would female bosses give commands then? Female bosses take advantage of the much softer commands often used by parents toward their children or by teachers toward their students. This command pattern consists of a verb stem followed by なさい. The ending なさい is the request form of the verb なさる "to do (honorific)."

言う	→	言いなさい	"Say it."
書く	→	書きなさい	"Write."
泳ぐ	→	泳ぎなさい	"Swim."
話す	→	話しなさい	"Talk."
待つ	→	待ちなさい	"Wait."
飲む	→	飲みなさい	"Drink."

帰る	→	帰りなさい	"Go home."
食べる	→	食べなさい	"Eat."
見る	→	見なさい	"Look."
来る	→	来なさい	"Come."
する	→	しなさい	"Do."

Parents may lecture their children using these command forms in the following manner:

起きなさい。
"Wake up."

歯をみがきなさい。
"Brush your teeth."

ちゃんと野菜も食べなさい。
"Eat vegetables, too, as you should."

宿題をしてから遊びなさい。
"Play after doing your homework."

This pattern is also used for textbook instructions or exam questions.

クラスメートと意見を交換しなさい。
"Share your opinions with your classmates."

重なった部分の面積を計算しなさい。
"Calculate the overlapping area."

正しい答えを選びなさい。
"Choose the correct answer."

間違っているものに×をつけなさい。
"Mark the wrong choices with 'x'."

The なさい-form, although not as stern as the imperative form, is still a firm command form and tends to signal an "I-know-better-than-you-what's-best-for-you" attitude. Thus, female bosses can resort to this pattern in order to give commands to their subordinate workers.

田中君、取引先に資料を送りなさい。
"Mr. Tanaka, send the information to the client."

木村さん、メーカーにすぐ連絡しなさい。
"Ms. Kimura, contact the manufacturer right away."

Like the brusque command forms, なさい-forms can be softened by adding the particle よ. The adjusted forms are used by female speakers. For instance, drinking after work, female office workers may speak as in the following:

もっと飲みなさいよ。
"Drink more."

ほんとのこと言いなさいよ。
"Tell me the truth."

たまにはおごりなさいよ。
"Pay for me sometimes."

The ending なさい may be truncated to な. In movies, this pattern is often associated with sage-like guardians guiding youths.

そこに座りな。
"Have a seat there."

人の話をよく聞きな。
"Listen to others carefully."

Do not confuse this pattern with the brusque negative commands we studied above, which require a plain non-past affirmative form.

そこに座るな。
"Do not sit there."

人の話を聞くな。
"Do not pay attention to others."

The negative version of なさい is なさんな, but it is not in common use. To give a negative command, female speakers rephrase it as an affirmative guardian's command or opt for other indirect expressions such as the prohibition form [V-て] はいけません (*see BJ* Unit 21).

大<ruby>き<rt>おお</rt></ruby>な<ruby>声<rt>こえ</rt></ruby>を<ruby>出<rt>だ</rt></ruby>すのはやめなさい。

"Stop speaking loud."

✓そこに<ruby>座<rt>すわ</rt></ruby>ってはいけません。

"You may not sit there."

Exercise 10.1

Translate the following traffic signs.

1. <ruby>自転車<rt>じてんしゃ</rt></ruby>も<ruby>止<rt>と</rt></ruby>まれ
2. ゆずれ
3. この<ruby>先<rt>さき</rt></ruby>カーブ、スピード<ruby>落<rt>お</rt></ruby>とせ
4. <ruby>危険<rt>きけん</rt></ruby>、<ruby>入<rt>はい</rt></ruby>るな
5. <ruby>危<rt>あぶ</rt></ruby>ない、<ruby>飛<rt>と</rt></ruby>び<ruby>出<rt>だ</rt></ruby>すな

Exercise 10.2

Change the following request forms to male speakers' friendly commands.

1. たまには、<ruby>付<rt>つ</rt></ruby>き<ruby>合<rt>あ</rt></ruby>って<ruby>下<rt>くだ</rt></ruby>さい。

   "Please go out with me from time to time."
2. もっと<ruby>食<rt>た</rt></ruby>べて<ruby>下<rt>くだ</rt></ruby>さい。

   "Please eat more."
3. からかうのはやめて<ruby>下<rt>くだ</rt></ruby>さい。

   "Please stop teasing me.
4. これ<ruby>以上<rt>いじょう</rt></ruby><ruby>飲<rt>の</rt></ruby>まないで<ruby>下<rt>くだ</rt></ruby>さい。

   "Please do not drink more."

Exercise 10.3

Change sentences 1–3 in 10.2 to female speakers' friendly commands.

Exercise 10.4

For each of the utterances in 1–4, choose the appropriate situation from
a–d.

1. 手^てをあげろ。   [   ]
2. 手^てをあげて下^{くだ}さい。 [   ]
3. 手^てをおあげ下^{くだ}さい。 [   ]
4. 手^てをあげなさい。   [   ]

a. A professor asking his students to raise their hands.

b. A mother asking her children to raise their hands.

c. A tour conductor asking a group of tourists to raise their hands.

d. A policeman ordering a suspect to raise his/her hands.

Exercise 10.5

Change the direct quote into the appropriate command form. You can
check the meaning of each sentence in the Key to exercises.

1. 私^{わたし}は守衛^{しゅえい}に「中^{なか}に入^{はい}らないで。」と言^いわれました。
   → 私は守衛^{しゅえい}に_____と言^いわれました。

2. 私^{わたし}は先生^{せんせい}に「もっと簡単^{かんたん}に説明^{せつめい}して下^{くだ}さい。」と言^いわれまし
   た。
   → 私^{わたし}は先生^{せんせい}に_____と言^いわれました。

3. 私^{わたし}は守衛^{しゅえい}に「大^{おお}きな声^{こえ}で話^{はな}さないで下^{くだ}さい。」と怒^{おこ}られまし
   た。
   → 私^{わたし}は守衛^{しゅえい}に_____と怒^{おこ}られました。

4. 私^{わたし}は高橋^{たかはし}さんに「一緒^{いっしょ}に行^いって下^{くだ}さい。」と頼^{たの}まれました。
   → 私^{わたし}は高橋^{たかはし}さんに_____と頼^{たの}まれました。

UNIT 11

Expressing desire for others to do something

Main target grammar in this unit

<ruby>君<rt>きみ</rt></ruby>に<ruby>話<rt>はな</rt></ruby>してほしい、<ruby>君<rt>きみ</rt></ruby>に<ruby>話<rt>はな</rt></ruby>してもらいたい

English grammar does not make a sharp distinction between one's desire to do something and one's desire for other people to do something. They are expressed using two apparently related constructions.

> I want to know the difference between right and wrong.
> I also want **you** to know the difference between right and wrong.

In Japanese, these two sentence types are expressed with two distinct constructions. In *BJ* Unit 15, we learned that the [V-stem] たい pattern is used for the first type, namely the desire for one's own action or change. In this unit, we will study how to express the second type of desire. Reflecting the added complexity of the meaning, the Japanese grammatical pattern needed to accomplish this task is slightly more complex than the [V-stem] たい pattern.

Using the adjective for desire: [V-て] ほしい

To express one's desire for other people to do something or undergo some change, the て-form of a verb and the い-**ADJECTIVE** ほしい "want" are combined, as in the following:

<ruby>笑<rt>わら</rt></ruby>ってほしい。
"I want you/her/him/them to smile/laugh."

102

✓幸せになってほしい。

"I want you/her/him/them to lead a happy life."

The adjective ほしい is directly attached to a て-form. No adverb or noun phrase can intervene between the て-form and ほしい. Here are some sentences with various additional phrases appearing in front of て-forms:

今日のこと、いつまでも覚えていてほしい。

"I want you to remember today forever."

ちょっと話を聞いてほしいんだけど、時間ある?

"I want you to listen to me. Do you have time?"

そういうことはもっとよく考えてから決めてほしいね。

"I want you to make a decision like that after giving it more careful thought."

ちょっと見てほしいものがあるんですが。

"I have something I want you to have a look at."

As the translations indicate, in a statement the subject of this type of sentence is usually the speaker, and, unless explicitly indicated otherwise, the person who is expected to do something or undergo some change is the listener. In a question, these roles are reversed.

何から始めてほしいですか。

"What do you want me to start with?"

Be sure not to use questions with [V-て] ほしい to someone who is socially higher than you. Use [V-stem] ましょうか instead (*see BJ* Unit 19).

何から始めましょうか。

"What should I start with?"

If you want to spell out the person who should perform the action, place a noun phrase standing for him/her somewhere before the て-form and mark it with the particle に. (See the similar uses of the particle に in the causative construction in Unit 20 and in the [V-て] もらう construction in *BJ* Unit 24. The property common to such uses of に is that the individual so marked is a non-subject agent.)

103

この仕事は君にしてほしい。
"I want you to do this job."

私に何をしてほしいの?
"What do you want me to do?"

親なら子供に幸せになってほしいと願うでしょう。
"Parents would wish that their children will live a happy life."

A に-phrase is not used if the desirable change concerns an impersonal situation.

明日は、晴れてほしい。
"I want it to become sunny tomorrow."

経済がよくなってほしい。
"I want the economy to improve."

The combination of a て-form and ほしい is conjugated like an adjective (*see* Appendix B and *BJ* Unit 6 for adjectival conjugation). The following table shows this with いてほしい "want you to be (here)" as an example.

Plain conjugation of [V-て] ほしい

	Affirmative	Negative
PLAIN		
Non-past	いてほしい "want you to to be here"	いてほしくない "do not want you to be here"
Past	いてほしかった "wanted you to be here"	いてほしくなかった "did not want you to be here"
POLITE		
Non-past	いてほしいです "want you to to be here"	いてほしくないです "do not want you to be here"

Past	いてほしかったです	いてほしくなかったです
	"wanted you to be here"	"did not want you to be here"

Additionally, you can use a negative て-form (usually of an action verb) in combination with an affirmative form of ほしい.

	Negative て-form + Affirmative ending
	PLAIN
Non-past	見^みないでほしい "want you not to look at it"
Past	見^みないでほしかった "wanted you not to look at it"

These combinations indicate that the subject positively hopes/hoped that the action will/would not be carried out, as exemplified by the following sentence:

そんなことは絶対^{ぜったい}に言^いわないでほしいです。
"I don't want you to say such a thing ever."

In contrast, the combination of an affirmative て-form of an action verb and a negative form of ほしい communicates a less assertive attitude, as exemplified by the following sentence. (*See* Unit 12 for similar contrasts involving つもり.)

本当^{ほんとう}は来^きてほしくなかったけど、そう言^いえなかった。
"To tell the truth, I didn't want him to come over, but I couldn't say so."

Using the [V-stem] たい-form of [V-て] もらう: [V-て] もらいたい

The other pattern that you can use to express your desire for someone else's action is [V-て] もらいたい. This form is the たい-form of [V-て] もらう "have someone to do something" that we studied in *BJ* Unit 24. Since

[V-て] もらう contains the sense that the action is beneficial to the subject, the [V-て] もらいたい option means that the subject (usually the speaker) wants someone else to do an action beneficial to him/her. However, in contemporary usage, this pattern is largely interchangeable with [V-て] ほしい.

幸せになってもらいたい。

"I want you/her/him/them to lead a happy life."

√ そんなことは絶対に言わないでもらいたいです。

"I don't want you to say such a thing ever."

Just like the [V-て] ほしい pattern, the person who is hoped to do the action is marked by に:

√重たいから力のある人に手伝ってもらいたいんですが。

"Since it is heavy, I want someone who is strong to help me."

This pattern, when combined with [P-plain^(na)] んですが, as shown above, is appropriate for asking for favors. 頂く, the humble version of もらう (*see BJ* Units 10 and 24) makes this pattern more polite and appropriate for formal requests for favor.

√写真を送って頂きたいのですが。

"I would like you to send me photos."

用意して頂きたいものをこのリストにまとめました。

"I summarized into this list the things that I would like you to prepare."

作り方をご存知の方にぜひ教えて頂きたいです。

"I would very much like someone who knows how to make it to teach me how."

The expression [V-て] 頂きたいです is functionally similar to the request forms [V-て] くれませんか/[V-て] 下さいませんか "won't you please" and [V-て] 頂けませんか "can I ask you to." For instance, the last sentence can be rephrased in the following manner:

作り方を知っている方、ぜひ教えてくれませんか。

"Those of you who know how to make it, won't you please tell me how?"

作り方をご存知の方、ぜひ教えて下さいませんか。

"Those of you who know how to make it, won't you please tell me how?"

作り方をご存知の方、ぜひ教えて頂けませんか。

"Those of you who know how to make it, can I ask you to tell me how?"

Exercise 11.1

Choose between [V-stem] たい and [V-て] ほしい and translate the sentence.

1. 私にお金があったら{買いたい/買ってほしい}のはこのモデルです。

2. 私の気持ちを{分かりたかった/分かってほしかった}けど、分かってくれなかった。

3. いっしょに{行きたい/行ってほしい}んだけど、時間ある?

4. {言いたい/言ってほしい}ことがあったら、はっきり{言いたい/言ってほしい}。

Exercise 11.2

Insert the appropriate particle that fits the translation. Do not use は.

1. 子供( )親( )一番してほしいのはこういうことだ。

   "What parents want their children to do most is this sort of thing."

2. 子供( )親( )言ってほしくないことはこういうことだ。

   "What children do not want their parents to say is this sort of thing."

3. 子供( )親( )自分を兄弟や友だちとくらべてほしくないのは当然だ。

   "It is natural for children to not want their parents to compare them with their siblings and friends."

Exercise 11.3

Translate the sentences into plain-style Japanese. You do not need to supply the personal pronouns.

1. What do you want me to make?

2. Which one do you want me to look at?

3. Who do you want me to meet?

4. At what time do you want me to come over (here)?

Exercise 11.4

Translate each request into English and rephrase it using (a) [V-て] 頂けませんか and (b) [V-て] 頂きたいのですが.

1. 必要なものを言って下さいませんか。 →

    (a) _____

    (b) _____

2. この書類を読んでコメントして下さいませんか。 →

    (a) _____

    (b) _____

Exercise 11.5

Using [V-て] 頂けませんか, complete the request for each situation.

1. When you want your professor to write a letter of recommendation (推薦状).

    _____

2. When you want a customer to fill out the form with his/her name, address (住所), and telephone number.

    _____

Exercise 11.6

Skim through the following message and summarize three things that this company representative wants the customer to do.

拝啓、毎度格別のお引き立てを 賜 り、厚く御礼申し
上げます。

さて、ご質問のありました商品の件ですが、チェッ
クリストを添付いたしますので、該当する項目をチェ
ックして 頂 けますでしょうか。その上で、お手数で
すが、責任者の山田(t-yamada@productservice.jp)宛、
記入済みのチェックリストをメールして 頂 ければ、
幸 いに存じます。その際、件名には、Q129HYと書
いて 頂 けると、幸 いです。

敬具

Exercise 11.7

Translate the following advice on how to write emails.

Eメールの上手な書き方1：Eメールを受け取った人
にちゃんと早く読んでほしかったら、件名は、それだ
けで内容が分かってもらえるように書きます。それか
ら、読んだ人にしてほしいことを、「【確認してくだ
さい】11/3の予定」のように【】の中にはっきり書き
ます。

UNIT 12
Expressing intentions

Main target grammar in this unit

<ruby>話<rt>はな</rt></ruby>そうと<ruby>思<rt>おも</rt></ruby>う、<ruby>話<rt>はな</rt></ruby>すつもりだ

Intentions are often made public and subsequently verified and negotiated. For instance, if a son tells his unprepared parents his intention to drop out of college, the parents will ask what he intends to do without a college degree. If a company announces its plan to overtake another company, those involved may attempt to verify the true intentions behind the announcement. In this unit we will study how to express intentions in Japanese.

Using the pattern [V-plain volitional] と<ruby>思<rt>おも</rt></ruby>う/<ruby>思<rt>おも</rt></ruby>っている

A Japanese speaker may use the volitional form of a verb followed by と<ruby>思<rt>おも</rt></ruby>う/<ruby>思<rt>おも</rt></ruby>っている to indicate that s/he is contemplating doing something.

volitional form of a verb + と<ruby>思<rt>おも</rt></ruby>う "I/you think of doing"

In *BJ* Unit 19 we studied volitional forms as suggestion forms for an action involving the listener. We give a quick summary below. (*See* Appendix B for more examples.)

To create the volitional form of a five-row verb, change the last syllable of the dictionary form to the corresponding *o*-row syllable (shown in bold below) and lengthen the vowel.

Volitional forms of five-row verbs

言<ruby>う<rt>い</rt></ruby>	→	言<ruby>おう<rt>い</rt></ruby>	"Let's say (it)!"
待<ruby>つ<rt>ま</rt></ruby>	→	待<ruby>とう<rt>ま</rt></ruby>	"Let's wait!"

For one-row verbs, delete る from the dictionary form and add よう.

Volitional forms of one-row verbs

食<ruby>べる<rt>た</rt></ruby>	→	食<ruby>べよう<rt>た</rt></ruby>	"Let's eat!"
寝<ruby>る<rt>ね</rt></ruby>	→	寝<ruby>よう<rt>ね</rt></ruby>	"Let's sleep!"

The volitional forms of the irregular verbs する "do" and 来る "come" are しよう and 来よう, respectively.

Volitional forms of irregular verbs

する	→	しよう	"Let's do (it)!"
来る	→	来よう	"Let's come (here)!"

Non-volitional verbs such as ある and 見える do not have volitional forms (*see* Unit 2).

The new pattern [V-plain volitional] と思う is used in the following way:

√ 明日からまたがんばろうと思う。
   "I will again do my very best starting tomorrow."

そのことについて話そうと思ったんだ。
   "I thought of talking to you about that."

お父さん、僕、大学をやめようと思います。
   "Father, I am thinking of quitting college."

You can also verify someone else's intention using this pattern.

√ 誰に相談しようと思うの?
   "Who do you think of consulting?"

何で仕事をやめようと思ったんだい?
   "Why did you think of quitting the job?"

√みなさんは、大学を出て何をしようと思いますか。
"What do you people intend to do after graduating from college?"

There is a restriction as to what can be the subject of these sentences. That is, the subject of the declarative sentence must be the speaker, and the subject of the question the listener. The third person cannot be the subject of either the declarative sentence or the question because the verb 思う "think" is an INTERNAL PROCESS VERB that only expresses the speaker's internal thought.

The previous pattern is used only if you have just thought of something or if your intention is timeless and firm. If you have been pondering for a while (and therefore there is a chance for you to waver), use the [V-て] いる counterpart (*see* Units 2 and 8) shown below:

> volitional form of a verb ＋ と思っている
> "am/is/are thinking of doing"

私、実は、この仕事を辞めて、ほかに仕事をみつけようと思っているんです。
"To tell you the truth, I am thinking of quitting this job and finding another job."

大学をやめたら、見習いシェフになろうと思っています。
"When I drop out of college, I am thinking of becoming a trainee chef."

自分の店を持とうと思っているんですか。
"Are you thinking of owning your own restaurant?"

Unlike the pattern with 思う, the subject of this pattern can be a third party or a corporate entity.

娘は、新しいビジネスを始めようと思っています。
"My daughter is thinking of beginning a new business."

この会社は、南アメリカに進出しようと思っています。
"This company is contemplating building market share in South America."

A related pattern without a verb, which is shown below, surfaces in very informal contexts for the purpose of conveying casual decisions. The っと part is the lengthened version of the QUOTATIVE PARTICLE と.

> volitional form of a verb ＋ っと

Here are a couple of examples:

これ、買おうっと。
"(I think) I'm going to buy this."

もうさっさと貯金使おうっと。
"(I think) I'm going to spend my savings without waiting."

Many sentences containing this pattern require no real audience. Solitary speakers may mumble them to gear up for a new activity.

映画でも見ようっと。
"(I think) I'm going to watch a movie (or something)."

さあ、寝ようっと。
"All right, (I think) I'm going to bed."

Concrete plan: [V-plain non-past] つもりだ

You can use the previous pattern [V-plain volitional] と思う/思っている so long as you are giving serious thought to the plan, even if you are not entirely committed to it. To report a firmer intention, use つもりだ "it is my intention," whose use of a noun modified by a plain non-past verb form adds the sense of concreteness and firm commitment. This pattern is also limited to volitional verbs.

> plain non-past form of a verb ＋ つもりだ "It is my intention that …"

Here are some example sentences:

出来るだけ早く計画を立てるつもりです。
"We intend to develop the plan as soon as possible."

明日は、何時の新幹線に乗るつもり？

"What time bullet train are you planning to get on tomorrow?"

あのことは誰にも言わないつもりでした。

"I intended not to talk about that to anyone."

The verb form can be positive or negative as the above examples demonstrate. The copula だ can be conjugated for politeness, tense, and negative/positive polarity. Therefore, in principle, sixteen conjugational variations are possible per verb. The following table shows half of them, the eight plain variations, using 読む "read" as an example.

Conjugation of つもりだ

		Affirmative	Negative
		AFFIRMATIVE VERB	
	Non-past	読むつもりだ "I intend to read it."	読むつもりじゃない "It is not my intention to read it."
	Past	読むつもりだった "I intended to read it."	読むつもりじゃなかった "It was not my intention to read it."
		NEGATIVE VERB	
	Non-past	読まないつもりだ "I intend not to read it."	読まないつもりじゃない "It is not my intention not to read it."
	Past	読まないつもりだった "I intended not to read it."	読まないつもりじゃなかった "It was not my intention not to read it."

The difference between the type made of the positive copula plus a negative verb and the type made of the negative copula plus a positive verb is subtle. The first type is used to indicate that the speaker consciously plans or has planned to refrain from doing something.

A: 今年日本に行くの？

"Are you going to Japan this year?"

B: ううん、行かないつもり。

"No, my plan is not to go."

The second is used to refute the suggestion or assumption that one plans or has planned to do something. (*See* Unit 11 for similar contrasts involving [V-て] ほしい.)

√そんなこと言うつもりじゃなかったんだ。

"I had no intention of saying such a thing."

Below are a few more examples of how to use the variations:

√木曜日から休みをとるつもりだったが、忙しくて、とれない。

"I intended to take a vacation from Thursday on, but I am busy and cannot do so."

√連絡しなかったのは、会わないつもりだったからです。

"I did not contact her because I intended not to meet her."

√日本政府はその問題をどう扱うつもりなのだろう。

"I wonder how the Japanese government intends to deal with the issue."

Because this is a pattern for firm intention, it is often used not only to verify the other's intention, but also to challenge the other.

会社は、どう事故の責任をとるつもりですか。

"How is the company going to shoulder the responsibility for the accident?"

The angry father of a college drop-out might shout in the following manner:

お前、大学出ないで何になるつもりなんだ！

"What are you going to become without graduating college?"

Exercise 12.1

Change the verbs in parentheses into the volitional form. You can check
the meaning of each sentence in the Key to exercises.

1. 新しいラップトップを(買う)と思っているんだけど、どのモ
   デルがいいかな。
2. 今晩は、早く(帰る)と思っていたんだけど、無理だった。
3. あとで(食べる)と思って、冷蔵庫に入れた。
4. 名前を (聞く)と思ったけど、聞けなかった。

Exercise 12.2

Select the most appropriate ending from a–f for each of the sentences 1–5.
Do not use the same ending more than once. You can check the meaning
of each completed sentence in the Key to exercises.

1. 一度は買おうと思ったけど
2. 家に電話しようと思ったけど
3. 早く寝ようと思ったけど
4. 寒いから帽子をかぶろうと思ったけど
5. 8時からその番組を見ようと思ったけど

a. レポートが終わらなかった。
b. 誰も来なかった。
c. 見つからなかった。
d. ちょっと前に停電になった。
e. あんまり高かったから、やめた。
f. 昼から忙しくて忘れた。

Exercise 12.3

Suppose that you are consulted about personal decisions. Following the example, ask a follow-up question according to the cue provided in the parentheses. You can check the meaning of each exchange in the Key to exercises.

Example
大学をやめようと思っているんですが。
(why?)
→ どうしてやめようと思っているんですか。

1. イギリスに留学しようと思っているんですが。

 (starting when?)

2. 新しい仕事を始めようと思っているんですが。

 (what kind?)

3. 東京に行こうと思っているんだけど。

 (when?)

4. 今の会社をやめようと思っているんだけど。

 (why?)

Exercise 12.4

Suppose that you hear from one of your Japanese roommates that she/he is planning a surprise party for the other roommate. Formulate five plain-style questions to ask her/him concerning the following details, using the volitional form.

1. When
2. Where
3. Who to invite
4. What to serve
5. What to get for a present

Exercise 12.5

Fill in the blanks with the appropriate form. You can check the meaning
of each dialog in the Key to exercises.

1. A: 彼に会うつもり?

    B: ううん、＿＿＿＿＿＿つもり。

2. A: どうしてお母さんの指輪、売ったんですか。

    B: 実は、はじめは、売るつもり＿＿＿＿＿＿んですけど、どう
    しても現金が必要だったんです。

3. A: 宿題が出ていませんね。

    B: 先生、すみません。昨日提出するつもり＿＿＿＿＿＿
    んですけど、忘れていたんです。

Exercise 12.6

Suppose that you are interviewing a representative of a Japanese
automobile company. Ask questions like the following to verify what
their plans are for the sale of their new luxury sedan. Use the vocabulary
list below and つもり.

1. In which countries do you intend to market it?

2. When do you intend to start selling it?

3. At about how much do you intend to price it?

4. Do you intend to terminate the sale of the old model?

販売する	"to market, sell"
販売	"sales"
～に価格を設定する	"to price at"
終了する	"to terminate"

UNIT 13

Expressing purposes and objectives

Main target grammar in this unit

話しに行く、話すのに5分かかる、話すために準備する、話せるように準備する、話して行く、話して来る、話しておく

To express purpose in English, it is standard practice to use "to" plus the infinitival form of a verb. Using this pattern, you might say for instance that you are "going to the library **to look for some books**," that you "need to show your ID **to get inside the library**," and that you "want to check out some books **to write a paper**."

Interestingly, Japanese distinguishes between these three types of purposes: an immediate goal of a movement, an instrument's utility, and the objective of a planned activity. In this unit, we will study the three types of purpose constructions corresponding to these three types. In addition, we will study constructions for more indirect objectives and implied purposes.

Immediate goal of movement: [V-stem] に{行く/来る/もどる}

The first type has the following form:

Immediate goal of movement

Agent = Subj.	Destination	Part.	Target action (V-stem)	Part.	Change-of-location V
私は	図書館	に/へ	本を返し	に	行った。
I went to the library to return a book.

119

In this construction, the main verb is limited to change-of-location verbs such as 行く "go," 来る "come," and もどる "return."

The pattern combines two different types of goals, the destination and the target action, each of which can appear alone in a sentence. The destination is marked by the goal particle に or へ.

図書館{に/へ}行った。
"I went to the library."

The target action is marked by the goal particle に. It is performed upon arrival at the destination and is represented by a single verb stem such as 借り "borrow," 読み "read," and 返し "return," possibly preceded by its grammatical object.

本を返しに行った。
"I went (somewhere) to return a book."

To formulate the full sentence, you combine the two types of goals. It does not matter which of the two types comes first.

図書館{に/へ}本を返しに行った。
"I went to the library to return a book."

本を返しに図書館{に/へ}行った。
"I went to the library to return a book."

Note that the location in this construction is included as the goal of the change-of-location verb rather than the location of the target activity; thus it cannot be marked by the particle で.

× 図書館で本を返しに行った。

Note also that you may not combine two or more verbs into the target action. That is, you cannot translate, for instance, "I went to the library to return a book and check out more books" using this construction. (*See* the section on ために later in this unit to formulate this type of sentence.)

The following construction has a verbal noun variant, in which a verbal noun such as 買い物 "shopping" and 勉強 "studying" appears in place of a verb stem:

Immediate goal of movement with verbal noun

Agent = Subj.	Destination	Part.	Target action (verbal noun)	Part.	Change-of-location V
私<ruby>わたし</ruby>は	図書館<ruby>としょかん</ruby>	に/へ	調<ruby>しら</ruby>べ物<ruby>もの</ruby>	に	行<ruby>い</ruby>った。
I went to the library for basic research.					

For this variant, too, the location and the activity can be switched around.

図書館{に/へ}調べ物に行った。
"I went to the library for basic research."

調べ物に図書館{に/へ}行った。
"I went to the library for basic research."

Instrument's utility: [V-plain non-past] のに

The second type of purpose construction has the following structure:

Instrument's utility

Target action (plain non-past)	Nominalizer	Part.	Instrumental predicate
図書館に入る	の	に	学生証がいる。
You need a student ID to get inside the library.			

A couple of more examples are given below:

コピー機<ruby>き</ruby>を使<ruby>つか</ruby>うのにカードがいる。
"We need a card to use the copier."

論文<ruby>ろんぶん</ruby>をコピーするのに1時間<ruby>いちじかん</ruby>かかった。
"It took an hour to copy the research papers."

A notable structural difference between the previous type and this construction is that the purpose phrase in this type consists of a plain-style sentence followed by the nominalizer の (studied in *BJ* Unit 11). However, the particle after the nominalizer is the goal particle に just as in the first construction.

A semantic difference between this and the first type is that the main predicate in this construction is "instrumental" in the sense that it represents *means*, such as a tool, material, time, or cost. Some examples of instrumental predicates are given below:

棚の上の本をとるのにはしごを使った。 [tool]
"I used a ladder to reach for the books on the shelf."

ちらしを印刷するのに黄色い紙を使った。 [material]
"I used yellow paper to print flyers."

人名辞典で名前をさがすのに時間がかかった。 [time]
"It took time to find the names using a biographical dictionary."

論文をコピーするのに3000円かかった。 [cost]
"It cost me ¥3000 to copy the research paper."

Just as in the case of the first type, you can also use a verbal noun for the target action.

Instrument's utility with a verbal noun

Target action (verbal noun)	Part.	Instrumental predicate
本の貸し出し	に	学生証がいる。
You need a student ID for checking out the books.		

論文のコピーに2000円かかった。
"It cost me ¥2000 to copy the papers."

資料の請求に1週間かかった。
"The retrieval of the requested documents took one week."

Objective of a planned activity: [volitional V-plain non-past] ために

Basic pattern

The last type uses the noun ため "sake" to introduce the purpose clause. The predicate describes a purposeful action or some type of effort.

Objective of a planned activity

Target action (Volitional V plain non-past)		Part.	Human effort
レポートを書く	ため	に	本を5冊借りた。
I checked out five books in order to write a class paper.			

Here are more examples:

試験の準備をするために図書館で徹夜した。
"I spent the night at the library without sleeping in order to prepare for the exam."

徹夜で勉強するためには、コーヒーを何杯も飲む。
"In order to study overnight without sleeping, I drink many cups of coffee."

Unlike the previous construction denoting a simple utilitarian connection between the means and the objective, the sentences expressed using this construction emphasize the effort or competence of a person trying to achieve a goal. Here are a few more examples:

日本へ行くために日本語を勉強した。
"I studied Japanese in order to go to Japan."

日本で仕事をするためには適応力がいる。
"In order to work in Japan, you need adaptability."

Regular nouns and verbal nouns can appear in this construction, too.

試験のために勉強した。
"I studied for the test."

123

試験の準備のために図書館で徹夜した。
"I spent the night at the library without sleeping in order to prepare for the exam."

Comparison with other purpose phrases

Sometimes, the contrast between the の-based and ため-based purpose clauses may not be very clear. In the example below, both の and ため can be used. The only subtle difference is that ため highlights the action as a conscious, goal-oriented action.

本を読む{の/ため}にめがねをかける。
"I {wear/put on} glasses to read a book."

Some ため-phrases may seem interchangeable with a stem-type purpose phrase.

本を返すために図書館に行った。
"I went to the library to return some books."

本を返しに図書館に行った。
"I went to the library to return some books."

However, some ため-phrases, such as the one in the following sentence, cannot be replaced by a stem-type purpose phrase at all:

大学に入るために塾に通った。
"In order to enter a college, I commuted to a cram school."
× 大学に入りに塾に通った。

This is because the target action does not take place immediately upon arrival at the destination. Likewise, the following sentence cannot be rephrased with a stem-phrase:

論文をさがして読むために、図書館に行った。
"In order to look for a paper and read it, I went to the library."
× 論文をさがして読みに、図書館に行った。

This is because the stem-type purpose phrase can take only one simple action as the target. If the objective is complex, you must use ため.

Non-purpose use of ために: [Non-volitional P-plain^(no/na)] ために

In all examples of ために so far, ために follows a plain non-past form of a volitional verb (see Unit 2) or a volitional verbal noun. If ために follows a predicate expressing a non-controllable event, the ために-clause means a reason or cause.

成績_{せいせき}が悪_{わる}いために、補修授業_{ほしゅうじゅぎょう}を受_うけている。

"Because my grades are bad, I am taking supplementary classes."

Because a past event is also non-controllable, a ために-clause containing a past event also means a reason or cause.

朝早_{あさはや}く試験_{しけん}があったために、よく寝_ねられなかった。

"Because I had an exam early in the morning, I couldn't sleep well."

Such uses of ために can be substituted with から or ので (*BJ* Unit 23).

成績_{せいせき}が悪_{わる}いから、補修授業_{ほしゅうじゅぎょう}を受_うけている。

"Because my grades are bad, I am taking supplementary classes."

朝早_{あさはや}く試験_{しけん}があったので、よく寝_ねられなかった。

"Because I had an exam early in the morning, I couldn't sleep well."

The reason/cause use of ために is quite formal, and から and ので are preferred in informal conversation.

When regular nouns and verbal nouns appear in this construction, the interpretation of the ために-clause depends on whether the **main clause** describes a controllable action. For example, in the first example below, the ために-clause means "**due to** an accident" because the main clause describes an uncontrollable event. On the other hand, the ために-clause in the second example means "**for** the pedestrians" because the main clause describes a controllable action.

事故_{じこ}のために渋滞_{じゅうたい}した。 [uncontrollable]

"(The road) became congested due to an accident."

歩行者_{ほこうしゃ}のために止_とまった。 [controllable]

"(The car) stopped for the pedestrians."

Indirect objectives: [non-volitional V/A-plain^(na) non-past] ように

In this section, we will study a construction that describes more indirect objectives than the three constructions we have studied so far. In this construction, ように follows the non-past plain form of a non-volitional verb or い/な-adjective. (*See also* Units 14 and 16 for special functions of ようになる and ように言う respectively.)

Indirect objectives

Target situation (non-volitional V/A plain^(na) non-past)		Action
黒板がよく見える	ように	前の方に座った。
I sat toward the front so that I could see the blackboard well.		

In this construction, the target situation is not under the volitional control of the main clause subject. Typically, the predicate inside the subordinate clause is non-volitional,

見えるように、〜　　　　"so that it is visible"

使えるように、〜　　　　"so that they can use it"

使いやすいように、〜　　"so that it is easy to use"

安全なように、〜　　　　"so that it is safe"

or, the subordinate clause subject being different from the main clause subject, the main clause subject cannot control the target situation.

田中さんが 〜 ように、私が〜
"So that Ms. Tanaka will ..., I ..."

For instance, in the following sentence, the student does not have volitional control over the outcome of the examination, and the subordinate clause predicate is non-volitional 落ちない "do not fail":

試験に落ちないように一生懸命勉強した。
"So that I will not fail the exam, I studied hard."

In the following example, the individual that posts the regulations (= 私) is different from those who are supposed to read them (= みんな):

（私は、）みんなが決まりを読むように、正面のドアにはった。
"So that everyone will read the regulations, I posted them on the front door."

The following example exemplifies both properties. The individual that posts the flyers is different from the examinees that need to locate the exam site, and the subordinate clause predicate is non-volitional:

試験会場がすぐ分かるようにエレベーターの中にも案内をはった。
"So that it is easy to find the examination site, we posted flyers inside elevators, too."

Implying purposes: [volitional V-て] {行く／来る／おく／ある}

The constructions that we have studied so far in this unit are used to indicate explicitly the purposes or objectives. You can also imply that an action has a purpose by using a number of patterns employing て-forms.

日本語の学生は、クラスに行く前に漢字を復習して行く。
"Students of Japanese review *kanji* before going to class."

日本語の学生は、クラスに来る前に漢字を復習して来る。
"Students of Japanese review *kanji* before coming to class."

日本語の先生は、学生が来る前に黒板に漢字を書いておく。
"The Japanese teacher writes *kanji* on the blackboard before the students come."

These patterns capitalize on the ability of て-forms to mark sequences and hence imply consequences: [V-て] 行く and [V-て] 来る suggest that an action has consequences for the destination or the people at the destination. In the first sentences above, students reviewing the materials has positive consequences for the effectiveness of the class, which is the implied purpose. Likewise, [V-て] おく suggests that one's present action has positive consequences for the future. Preparedness is the implied purpose.

The pattern [V-て] ある that we studied in Unit 8 is an intransitive counter part of [V-て] おく and also implies preparedness.

<ruby>黒板<rt>こくばん</rt></ruby>に<ruby>漢字<rt>かんじ</rt></ruby>が<ruby>書<rt>か</rt></ruby>いてある。

"*Kanji* have been written on the blackboard (in preparation)."

(*See* Unit 14 for [non-volitional V-て] <ruby>来<rt>く</rt></ruby>る that describes an inception.)

Exercise 13.1

Fill in the blanks with the appropriate purpose expression containing a stem form.

1. <ruby>明日<rt>あした</rt></ruby>はパンダを＿＿＿＿＿＿<ruby>動物園<rt>どうぶつえん</rt></ruby>へ<ruby>行<rt>い</rt></ruby>きます。

   "Tomorrow, I will go to the zoo to see a panda."

2. <ruby>友<rt>とも</rt></ruby>だちが<ruby>私<rt>わたし</rt></ruby>に＿＿＿＿＿＿<ruby>来<rt>き</rt></ruby>ました。

   "A friend of mine came to see me."

3. <ruby>財布<rt>さいふ</rt></ruby>を＿＿＿＿＿＿<ruby>家<rt>うち</rt></ruby>に<ruby>帰<rt>かえ</rt></ruby>りました。

   "I went home to get my wallet."

4. <ruby>何<rt>なに</rt></ruby>を＿＿＿＿＿＿<ruby>来<rt>き</rt></ruby>たの?

   "What did you come to do?" (= What brought you here?)

Exercise 13.2

Translate the following sentences into Japanese using のに.

1. How much does it cost to go to Tokyo flying economy class?

2. How long does it take to go to Tokyo by direct flight (<ruby>直行便<rt>ちょっこうびん</rt></ruby>)?

3. What will I need to buy a ticket?

4. What should I use to wrap the wine bottle?

5. Where should I go to check in (for a flight)?

Exercise 13.3

Fill in the blanks with appropriate purpose expressions and translate the passage.

日本では、大学に入る(　　　)に、誰でも大学入試センター試験という試験を受ける。この試験は、毎年一月ごろにあって、東京や大阪には、たくさんの高校生や予備校生が試験を受け(　　　)来る。ホテルはそんな学生の(　　　)に特別の料理を出したり、勉強の(　　　)のスペースを作ったりする。試験を受ける(　　　)には、ずいぶんお金がかかりそうだ。

Exercise 13.4

Connect matching halves from 1–6 and a–f with ように, adjusting the forms of 1–6 appropriately.

1. 会議に間に合います
2. かぜをひきません
3. お弁当を忘れません
4. 先生の話がよく聞こえます
5. 寒くありません
6. 座って行けます

a. タクシーに乗りました
b. 指定席を予約しておきます
c. 毎日うがいをします
d. マフラーをして行きます
e. かばんに入れておきます
f. 一番前の席に座ります

Exercise 13.5

Choose between のに, ために, and ように.

1. 歯が白くなる{のに/ために/ように}特別の歯磨きを使いました。
2. 歯をみがく{のに/ために/ように}は、やわらかい歯ブラシがいいです。
3. 歯を白くする{のに/ために/ように}毎日ていねいにみがきました。
4. 歯をみがく{のに/ために/ように}10分ぐらいかかります。

Exercise 13.6

Using [V-て] おいて(ください), formulate instructions appropriate for the following situations.

1. A female boss needs to have two extra printer cartridges ordered.

2. A housemate wants his/her housemate to put out the trash before 6 a.m.

3. A teacher wants his/her students to read a newspaper article so that they can discuss it in the next class.

4. A housemate wants his/her housemate to go buy laundry detergent (洗濯石けん).

UNIT 14

Describing change

Main target grammar in this unit

１５才になる、背が高くなる、話さなくなる、話すようになる、話すことになる、話し始める

A thirteenth-century literary work known as 方丈記 begins with a passage to the effect that every worldly thing is ephemeral and must change just as a river that appears to follow a constant path is changing. Such philosophical and aesthetic appreciation of natural transition is echoed linguistically in Japanese. There are numerous linguistic patterns that center on the concept of change. In this unit, we will study some such patterns that are used to describe change of weather, transition between seasons, life cycles, etc. We will also compare these patterns with some similar or related patterns.

Changes in state: [N/A-adverbial] なる

To express a non-volitional change from one state to another, such as seasonal, economic, social, and historical changes, as well as a transition in an individual's life, use the adverbial form of a noun predicate or い/な-adjective followed by the verb なる, as shown below:

Changes in state

What undergoes change = Subj./topic	End result (N/A-adverbial)	V
子どもが	５才に/ 静かに/大きく	なった。
The child turned 5/became quiet/grew up (bigger).		

131

Think of this pattern in the following manner. When, for instance, a child turns five, quiets down, or has grown bigger, the end results would be expressed as in the following:

5才だ。　　　　　　　　　　[noun predicate]
"S/he is five years old."

静かだ。　　　　　　　　　　[な-adjective]
"S/he is quiet."

大きい。　　　　　　　　　　[い-adjective]
"S/he is big."

To describe the change to these conditions, turn the predicates into their adverbial forms and add the verb なる "become." The adverbial form of a noun predicate or a な-adjective is created by dropping だ and adding に.

Noun/な-adjective pattern

5才[だ → に] + なる	5才になる。 "S/he becomes five."
静か[だ → に] + なる	静かに なる。 "S/he becomes quiet."

The adverbial form of an い-adjective is created by replacing い with く.

い-adjective pattern

大き[い → く]+なる	大きくなる。 "S/he becomes big."

For いい "good," use the irregular く-form よく.

よく なる。
"It becomes good."

Here are some contextualized examples. Note that each of them contains the noun/な-adjective pattern and the い-adjective pattern:

来年は、大学を出て、社会人になる。朝が早くなるだろう。
"Next year, graduating from college, I will become a company
employee. The (time I get up in the) morning will become earlier."

春になりました。日が長くなりました。
"It has become spring. (= Spring has come.) The day has become
long."

２０年前ドイツが一つになった。ベルリンの壁がなくなった。
"Germany became one 20 years ago. (= Germany became unified 20
years ago.) The Berlin Wall ceased to exist."

１ユーロ100円になって、ヨーロッパの物が高くなった。
"(The exchange rate) has become ¥100 to a Euro, and European things
have become expensive."

息子は高校生になって、声が低くなった。
"My son became a high school student, and his voice became low."

Applications of the い-adjective pattern

The predicate that appears in the い-adjective pattern is not limited to
plain adjectives. All い-adjective type predicates including negative forms
and **COMPOUND ADJECTIVES** can appear in this pattern.

Variations of the い-adjective pattern

	Target condition	Change to the target
Negative noun predicate	学生じゃない "not a student"	学生じゃなくなる "stop being a student"
Negative な-adjective	便利じゃない "not convenient"	便利じゃなくなる "stop being convenient"
Negative い-adjective	安くない "not cheap"	安くなくなる "stop being cheap"

Compound い-adjective	会<ruby>会<rt>あ</rt></ruby>いたい "want to meet"	会<ruby>会<rt>あ</rt></ruby>いたくなる "begin to want to meet"
	食<ruby>食<rt>た</rt></ruby>べやすい "easy to eat"	食<ruby>食<rt>た</rt></ruby>べやすくなる "become easy to eat"
	使<ruby>使<rt>つか</rt></ruby>いにくい "difficult to use"	使<ruby>使<rt>つか</rt></ruby>いにくくなる "become difficult to use"
Negative form of a compound い-adjective	会<ruby>会<rt>あ</rt></ruby>いたくない "not want to meet"	会<ruby>会<rt>あ</rt></ruby>いたくなくなる "lose interest in meeting"
Negative verb	分<ruby>分<rt>わ</rt></ruby>からない "not understand"	分<ruby>分<rt>わ</rt></ruby>からなくなる "get confused"
Negative potential form	食<ruby>食<rt>た</rt></ruby>べられない "cannot eat"	食<ruby>食<rt>た</rt></ruby>べられなくなる "can no longer eat"

Here are some example sentences:

その<ruby>人<rt>ひと</rt></ruby>のよくないうわさを<ruby>聞<rt></rt></ruby>いて、<ruby>会<rt>あ</rt></ruby>いたくなくなりました。

"Hearing unsavory rumors about him, I became reluctant to meet him."

<ruby>暗<rt>くら</rt></ruby>くなって、<ruby>道<rt>みち</rt></ruby>が<ruby>分<rt>わ</rt></ruby>からなくなった。おまけに<ruby>雨<rt>あめ</rt></ruby>で<ruby>前<rt>まえ</rt></ruby>が<ruby>見<rt>み</rt></ruby>えなくなって、<ruby>運転出来<rt>うんてんでき</rt></ruby>なくなった。

"It became dark, and I got lost. To make the matter worse, because of the rain, it became impossible to see the area ahead, and I could no longer drive."

おじいちゃんは、<ruby>歯<rt>は</rt></ruby>が<ruby>悪<rt>わる</rt></ruby>くなってから、かたい<ruby>物<rt>もの</rt></ruby>が<ruby>食<rt>た</rt></ruby>べられなくなったんだ。

"After his teeth became bad, it became impossible for Grandpa to eat hard things."

These sentences are somewhat difficult to translate into English because English does not have a standard pattern or verb for expressing such changes in state. If you need to translate such sentences into English, it is worth experimenting with various alternatives to bring out the sense of change. For example, adding an expression such as "no longer" may sometimes work.

Habitual changes: [V-plain non-past] ようになる

If you want to say that someone has begun to do something habitually, use the following pattern.

Habitual changes

What undergoes change = Subj./topic	Changed action		V
子どもが	野菜を食べる	ように	なる。
The child begins to eat vegetables.			

This construction consists of a subordinate clause, the adverbial form of よう "condition, appearance," ように (*see* Units 13, 15, and 16 for other uses of よう), and the verb なる. Therefore, it literally means "reach the condition where one does something."

Here are more example sentences. The habitual changes can be about human as well as non-human entities:

どんなに寒くても毎朝ジョギングをするようになった。
"I began to go jogging every morning however cold it may be."

花をバルコニーに植えてから蝶が来るようになった。
"Since I planted flowers in the balcony, butterflies started to come."

最近飛行機が家の上を飛ぶようになった。
"Airplanes have begun to fly above my house recently."

A change to a negative condition, particularly a conscious change, can be expressed using the non-past negative form of a verb before ようになる.

ファストフードの店に行かないようになった。
"I stopped going to fast-food restaurants."

A change to a negative condition can also be expressed using the negative form of an action verb in the い-adjective pattern that we studied earlier.

Negative form of an action verb in the い-adjective pattern

	Target condition	Change to the target
Negative noun predicate	食^たべない "not eat"	食^たべなくなる "come to stop eating"
Negative な-adjective	使^{つか}わない "not use"	使^{つか}わなくなる "come to stop using"

Here are some example sentences:

塩^{しお}を使^{つか}わなくなってから、血圧^{けつあつ}が低^{ひく}くなった。
"After I stopped using salt, my blood pressure went down."

みんなが毎日^{まいにち}食^たべなくなって、卵^{たまご}が売^うれなくなった。
"Most people stopped eating eggs every day, and the sale of eggs dropped."

Controllability: なる **versus** する

So far, we have used なる "become" as the main predicate. For every sentence that we have studied so far, there is a corresponding sentence with する "do." Although the なる version has the sense that the change happens, the する version has the sense that the change is induced by an individual under his/her control. In other words, the なる version is intransitive, whereas the する version is transitive (*see also* Unit 2). Compare some paired phrases:

安^{やす}くなる
"become cheap"

安^{やす}くする
"will make it cheap"

食^たべやすくなる
"become easy to eat"

食^たべやすくする
"will make it easy to eat"

読^よむようになる
"begin to read habitually"

読^よむようにする
"will make sure that someone reads it"

Here are a few contextualized sentences containing する:

このコピーは見^みにくいですね。もっと大^{おお}きくしてください。
"This copy is difficult to see. Please make it larger."

明日^{あした}は、面接^{めんせつ}だから、今晩^{こんばん}は、早^{はや}く寝^ねるようにするね。
"Since I have a job interview tomorrow, I will make sure to go to bed early tonight."

健康^{けんこう}のために、毎日^{まいにち}、隣^{となり}の駅^{えき}まで歩^{ある}くようにしています。
"I am making sure to walk to the next station every day for my health."

Patterns for decision making: [V-plain non-past] ことになる/[V-plain non-past] ことにする

Next we will study two more patterns that are structurally related to the patterns we have studied so far: a non-past plain verb followed by ことになる and ことにする.

こと is an abstract nominalizer (*see BJ* Unit 11). [V-plain non-past] ことになる means "come to the conclusion that ..." or "be decided that ..."

4月^{しがつ}にロンドンで結婚^{けっこん}することになりました。
"It has been decided that we will get married in London in April."

[V-plain non-past] ことにする "decide to" is more active than [V-plain non-past] ことになる because of the main verb する "do."

まだ他^{ほか}に誰^{だれ}にも言^いっていないんだけど、実^{じつ}は彼女^{かのじょ}と結婚^{けっこん}することにしたんだ。
"I haven't told this to anyone else yet, but to tell you the truth, I've decided to get married with her."

Of these two types, the なる option is considered more formal because it presents a decision as something (so significant that it is) beyond human control. Hence, important decisions are usually made public using this option. The する option is reserved for casual decisions or for private contexts.

Habitual change versus inception: [V-plain non-past] ようになる versus [V-stem] 始める

Above, we said that [V-plain non-past] ようになる means a change from a certain state to another. Specifically, if you use an action verb, the sentence means that a different habit or condition is formed, as shown below:

男は、たばこを吸うようになった。
"The man began to smoke."

This sentence can be translated successfully into English using the expression "begin to …" However, note that the resultant English translation does not necessarily mean that a habitual change has taken place. The individual may have just begun to smoke at that moment or may have begun to smoke habitually. In contrast, the Japanese expression 吸うようになる unambiguously means that a habitual change has taken place.

If you just want to focus on the inception of an action, use the pattern [V-stem] 始める. This is the closest Japanese counterpart of the English expression "begin to …" The following sentence is as ambiguous between the two readings as the English counterpart:

男は、たばこを吸い始めた。
"The man began to smoke."

A couple more examples are given below:

では、答えを書き始めて下さい。
"Well, then, please begin to write the answers."

ベッドでテレビを見始めたが、すぐ眠たくなった。
"She began to watch the TV in bed, but she soon became sleepy."

The other pattern used to describe an inception is [non-volitional V-て] 来る. (*See* Unit 13 for [volitional V-て] 来る, which implies purpose.) It means that something comes into the sensory field of the speaker. The verbs that combine with this pattern are more restricted than those that combine with 始める. First, something may come into view or come within earshot of the speaker.

山が見えて来ました。
"The mountains came into view."

空が曇って来ました。
"Clouds began to overcast the sky."

雨が降って来ました。
"It started to rain."

川の音が聞こえて来ました。
"The sound of the river came within earshot."

Or the speaker may feel something internally.

分かって来た。
"It started to make sense."

うれしくなって来た。
"I started to feel happy."

おなかがすいて来た。
"I started to feel hungry."

頭が痛くなって来た。
"I started to feel a headache."

Exercise 14.1

Fill in the right column with the corresponding expressions of change that contain the verb なる. You can check the meaning of each answer in the Key to exercises.

Target condition	Change to the target
安_{やす}い	
いい	
使_{つか}わない	
知_しりたい	
覚_{おぼ}えやすい	
静_{しず}かだ	
大学生_{だいがくせい}だ	
雪_{ゆき}だ	

Exercise 14.2

Following the example, fill in the blanks with the appropriate form. You can check the meaning of each triplet of sentences in the Key to exercises.

Example

前_{まえ}は便利_{べんり}じゃなかった。でも、(**便利_{べんり}に**)なった。今便利_{いまべんり}だ。
"It was not convenient before. However, it has become convenient. It is convenient now."

1. 前_{まえ}はあんまり忙_{いそが}しくなかった。でも、(　　　)なった。
今忙_{いまいそが}しい。

2. 朝_{あさ}は寒_{さむ}くなかった。でも、昼_{ひる}から(　　　)なった。今寒_{いまさむ}い。

3. 先学期_{せんがっき}は友_{とも}だちじゃなかった。でも、今学期_{こんがっき}(　　　)
なった。今友_{いまとも}だちだ。

4. 前_{まえ}は日本_{にほん}に行_いきたくなかった。でも、日本語_{にほんご}を勉強_{べんきょう}してから
(　　　)なった。今_{いま}とても行_いきたい。

5. 公衆電話がちょっと前までここにもあったが、知らないうちに
   (　　　　) なった。今どこにもない。

6. 前は買いたかったが、コメントを読んで (　　　　　　) なった。今
   は、ぜんぜん買いたくない。

Exercise 14.3

Following the example, fill in the blanks with an appropriate expression
and translate the sentence.

Example

携帯のカメラを(**使うように**)なって、デジカメを使わなくな
った。

"I began to use my cell phone's camera and stopped using my digital
camera."

1. 昔はアメリカ人はうすいコーヒーを飲んだが、２０年ぐらい
   前からこいコーヒーを (　　　) なった。

2. オンラインで買い物を (　　　) なって、あまりデパートに行か
   なくなった。

3. 携帯で時間を (　　　) なって、腕時計をしなくなった。

4. 窓のそばにえさ箱を置いたら、たくさん小鳥が (　　　) なった。

Exercise 14.4

Formally announce the following life-changing events.

1. You are going to enter a graduate school.

2. You are going to work for a Japanese company.

3. You are going to get married in June.

4. You are going to move to London.

Exercise 14.5

Choose the most appropriate form. You can check the meaning of each sentence in the Key to exercises.

1. この地方では、昔は毎年桜が4月に咲いたが、10年ぐらい前から、毎年3月に{咲くようになった/咲き始めた/咲いて来た}。

2. 川の近くの桜が{咲くようになった/咲き始めた/咲いて来た}そうですから、週末にいっしょに見に行きませんか。

3. では、テストの時間です。1ページ目の説明から{読むようになって/読み始めて/読んで来て}下さい。

4. もうすぐホテルに着くよ。ほら、あそこに海が{見えるようになった/見え始めた/見えて来た}。

UNIT 15

Estimating the likelihood of an event

Main target grammar in this unit

話<small>はな</small>すだろう、話<small>はな</small>すかもしれない、話<small>はな</small>しそうだ、話<small>はな</small>すようだ、
話<small>はな</small>すみたいだ、話<small>はな</small>すらしい、話<small>はな</small>すはずだ

English speakers resort to various expressions of conjecture that reflect different degrees of certainty, as, for example, in the following:

{Maybe/Probably/Surely}, it's going to rain.

It {could/might/will} rain.

{It looks like/I am sure that} it is going to rain.

Similarly, the Japanese language provides speakers with various methods for making conjectures, some of which we will study in this unit.

Adverbs that express degrees of certainty:

もしかしたら/たぶん/きっと/どうやら/たしか

As in English, a Japanese speaker can express an event's likelihood using an adverb. Here are some frequently used adverbs, each with a different degree of certainty:

もしかしたら	"perhaps, possibly"
たぶん	"probably"
きっと	"certainly, surely"
どうやら	"seemingly"
たしか	"if I recall correctly"

143

Here are some example sentences:

もしかしたら明日<ruby>明日<rt>あした</rt></ruby>は雨<ruby>雨<rt>あめ</rt></ruby>だ。
"Possibly it will rain tomorrow."

たぶん週末<ruby>週末<rt>しゅうまつ</rt></ruby>までには晴<ruby>晴<rt>は</rt></ruby>れる。
"It will probably clear up by the weekend."

きっと今年<ruby>今年<rt>ことし</rt></ruby>の夏<ruby>夏<rt>なつ</rt></ruby>も暑<ruby>暑<rt>あつ</rt></ruby>くなる。
"Surely it will be hot this summer again."

どうやら天気予報<ruby>天気予報<rt>てんきよほう</rt></ruby>は外<ruby>外<rt>はず</rt></ruby>れた。
"It seems like the weather forecast had it wrong."

たしか昨日<ruby>昨日<rt>きのう</rt></ruby>は最高気温<ruby>最高気温<rt>さいこうきおん</rt></ruby>が8度<ruby>度<rt>はちど</rt></ruby>でした。
"If I am not mistaken, the highest temperature yesterday was 8 °C."

Although they can stand alone as in the previous examples, more often than not these adverbs are accompanied by estimation forms, such as だろう "I suppose" and かもしれない "it may be," or adjectives of conjecture, such as はずだ "it is my understanding" and ようだ "it appears."

もしかしたら明日<ruby>明日<rt>あした</rt></ruby>は雨<ruby>雨<rt>あめ</rt></ruby>かもしれない。
"Possibly it might rain tomorrow."

たぶん週末<ruby>週末<rt>しゅうまつ</rt></ruby>までには晴<ruby>晴<rt>は</rt></ruby>れるだろう。
"I suppose it will probably clear up by the weekend."

きっと今年<ruby>今年<rt>ことし</rt></ruby>の夏<ruby>夏<rt>なつ</rt></ruby>も暑<ruby>暑<rt>あつ</rt></ruby>くなるだろう。
"I suppose it will surely be hot this summer again."

どうやら天気予報<ruby>天気予報<rt>てんきよほう</rt></ruby>は外<ruby>外<rt>はず</rt></ruby>れたようだ。
"It seems like the weather forecast had it wrong."

たしか昨日<ruby>昨日<rt>きのう</rt></ruby>は最高気温<ruby>最高気温<rt>さいこうきおん</rt></ruby>が8度<ruby>度<rt>はちど</rt></ruby>だったはずだ。
"If I am not mistaken, the highest temperature yesterday was 8 °C."

We will now study these endings more closely.

Estimation forms

The estimation forms simply express the degree of a speaker's commitment to the conjecture without giving any insight into how s/he has arrived at it.

Avoiding assertion: [P-plain^(da-drop)] だろう

The ending だろう is comparable to "I suppose that … /It is probably the case that …" Its polite counterpart is でしょう.

明日は暖かくなるだろう。 [plain]
"I suppose tomorrow will be warm."

明日は暖かくなるでしょう。　　[polite]
"I suppose tomorrow will be warm."

だろう does not conjugate for polarity or tense. In order to make a negative conjecture, change the predicate that precedes だろう into a negative form.

明日は寒くないだろう。
"I suppose tomorrow will not be cold."

Likewise, change the predicate that precedes だろう into a past form to present a conjecture about a past event or state.

昨日は東北でも暖かっただろう。
"I suppose that it was also warm in the Tohoku region yesterday."

In principle, だろう attaches to a plain-style form. However, the だ-form of the copula must be dropped before だろう because it has a strong sense of assertion and does not combine well with estimation forms in general (*see also* Unit 7).

The following table summarizes the conjugation patterns of predicates before だろう.

Conjugation patterns with だろう

Plain-style verb	雨が降る "it rains" 雨が降らない 雨が降った 雨が降らなかった	
い-adjective	暑い "(it) is hot" 暑くない 暑かった 暑くなかった	[plain] だろう
な-adjective	さわやかだ "(it) is refreshing" さわやかじゃない さわやかだった さわやかじゃなかった	[polite] でしょう
Noun	晴れだ "(it) is a sunny day" 晴れじゃない 晴れだった 晴れじゃなかった	

Since the degree of certainty is relatively high with だろう, it is more compatible with adverbs such as たぶん "probably" and きっと "certainly, surely" than もしかしたら "perhaps."

○ {たぶん/きっと}明日は雪でしょう。
   "I suppose it will probably/surely snow tomorrow."

× もしかしたら明日は雪でしょう。
   "I suppose it will perhaps snow tomorrow."

Because its primary function is to avoid strong assertion, だろう is also used as a politeness strategy in making a suggestion or asking for approval (*see BJ* Unit 21).

傘を持っていった方がいいでしょうね。 [suggestion]
"It will probably be better if you take an umbrella."

この傘を借りてもいいでしょうか。 [approval-seeking question]
"May I borrow this umbrella?"

Talking about possibility: [P-plain^(da-drop)] かもしれない

The ending かもしれない "there is a possibility that … /it might be that ..."
and its polite form かもしれません indicate that a certain event is at least
possible.

明日は雨が降るかもしれない。 [plain]
"It might rain tomorrow."

明日は雨が降るかもしれません。 [polite]
"It might rain tomorrow."

かもしれない indicates a lesser degree of certainty than だろう. Therefore, it
occurs with the adverb もしかしたら "possibly," but not with たぶん
"probably" or きっと "certainly, surely."

o　もしかしたら明日は雨かもしれません。
　　"It might rain tomorrow."

×　{たぶん/きっと}明日は雨かもしれません。

Like だろう, かもしれない generally follows a predicate in its plain form,
except that the だ-form of the copula is dropped.

Conjugation patterns with かもしれない

Plain-style verb	雨が降る "it rains" 雨が降らない 雨が降った 雨が降らなかった	[plain] かもしれない かもしれなかった
い-adjective	暑い "(it) is hot" 暑くない 暑かった 暑くなかった	[polite] かもしれません かもしれませんでした

な-adjective	さわやかだ "(it) is refreshing"	
	さわやかじゃない	
	さわやかだった	
	さわやかじゃなかった	
Noun	晴れだ "(it) is a sunny day"	
	晴れじゃない	
	晴れだった	
	晴れじゃなかった	

Although かもしれない contains しれない, the negative form of the verb しれる "be known," it does not indicate a negative conjecture, nor does it have an affirmative counterpart. That is, just like だろう, it does not conjugate for polarity. In order to make a negative conjecture, change the predicate that precedes かもしれない into a negative form.

明日は雨が**降らない**かもしれない。
"It might not rain tomorrow."

However, unlike だろう, かもしれない can conjugate for tense. Using かもしれなかった, you can indicate that an event or situation was deemed possible in the past.

嵐になる**かもしれなかった**。
"It looked like a storm could come."

かもしれない can also be used as a politeness strategy in making a suggestion.

傘を持っていった方がいい**かもしれませんね**。 [suggestion]
"It might be better to take an umbrella."

On the other hand, unlike だろう, かもしれない is seldom used in a question. Nor is it used as a politeness strategy when seeking approval.

× この傘を借りてもいいかもしれませんか。
(*intended*: "May I borrow this umbrella?")

Auxiliary adjectives of conjecture

In addition to the estimation forms we studied above, Japanese has a range of auxiliary adjectives that provide the information as to how the speaker has arrived at the conclusion. Below, we will study each of them carefully.

Intuitive judgment: [V/A-stem] そうだ₁

When そうだ₁ attaches to a verbal or adjectival stem form, it expresses the speaker's intuitive judgment based on some firsthand sensory information. When combined with an eventive predicate (*see* Unit 2), the conjecture is about a future event, whereas when combined with a stative predicate (*see* Unit 2), the conjecture is about the current state.

雨が降りそうだ。   [future event]
"It looks like it's about to rain."

北海道の冬は寒そうだ。   [current state]
(Looking at the TV) "Hokkaido's winter looks cold."

The range of forms to which そうだ₁ is attached is limited. It attaches only to verbal and adjectival stem forms. There is no noun form to which そうだ₁ can attach. However, そうだ₁ itself conjugates fully like a な-adjective for tense, polarity, and politeness, as shown in the following table:

Conjugation patterns with そうだ₁

Plain-style verb	雨が降り "to rain" 雨が降らな	[plain] そうだ そうじゃない そうだった
い-adjective	暑 "hot" 暑くなさ	そうじゃなかった [polite] そうです
な-adjective	さわやか "refreshing" さわやかじゃなさ	そうじゃありません (or そうじゃないです) そうでした そうじゃありませんでした (or そうじゃなかったです)

Many speakers treat regular い-adjectives such as 暑い and the non-past negative forms of verbs such as 降らない in the same manner before そうだ₁: they delete final い from both types and attach そうだ₁. (The acceptability of this pattern for verbs varies depending on the speaker and the verb.)

午後は暑そうだ。雨は降らなそうだ。

"It looks like it's going to be hot this afternoon. It doesn't look like it's going to rain."

The adjectives よい (いい) "good" and ない "absent" behave slightly differently. They drop い and have さ inserted before そうだ₁.

天気は、よさそうだ。雲はなさそうだ。

"The weather looks fine. It looks like there is no cloud."

This pattern is regularly used for non-past negative forms of い- and な-adjectives such as 暑くない and さわやかじゃない.

沖縄の冬は寒くなさそうだ。

(Looking at the TV) "Okinawa's winter looks not cold."

Because it cannot follow any tensed form, そうだ₁ cannot be used to express the speaker's conjecture concerning a past event or state. However, you can report on a conjecture made in the past by changing そうだ₁ to a past-tense form.

今にも雨が降りそうでした。

"It looked like it was about to rain any minute."

Do not confuse this そうだ₁, which attaches to a stem form of verbs and adjectives, with the hearsay そうだ₂, which follows a plain form of any types of predicates. *See* Unit 16 for the latter.

北海道の冬は寒そうです。   [V/A-stem そうだ₁]

"Hokkaido's winter looks cold."

北海道の冬は寒いそうです。   [P-plain そうだ₂]

"I heard that Hokkaido's winter is cold."

Inference: [P-plain^(no/na)] ようだ and [P-plain^(da-drop)]
みたいだ/らしい

ようだ is used to express the speaker's rational conjecture. Unlike in the case of そうだ₁, the source of conjecture is not limited to firsthand sensory information. For example, the following may be uttered either when the speaker sees a dark cloud spreading over the sky or when s/he has heard the weather forecast for a strong possibility of rain.

雨が降るようです。

"It appears that it will rain."

All predicate types appear before ようだ in their appropriate noun modification forms. ようだ itself conjugates like a な-adjective.

Conjugation patterns with ようだ

Plain-style verb	雨が降る "it rains" 雨が降らない 雨が降った 雨が降らなかった	[plain] ようだ ようじゃない ようだった ようじゃなかった
い-adjective	暑い "(it) is hot" 暑くない 暑かった 暑くなかった	
な-adjective	さわやかな "(it) is refreshing" さわやかじゃない さわやかだった さわやかじゃなかった	[polite] ようです ようじゃありません (or ようじゃないです) ようでした ようじゃありませんでした (or ようじゃなかったです)
Noun	晴れの "(it) is a sunny day" 晴れじゃない 晴れだった 晴れじゃなかった	

Notably, this form can be used to express the speaker's conjecture concerning a past event or state. For example, you may utter the following sentence when you see a paddle on the ground after coming out of a subway station.

雨が降ったようだ。

"It appears that it has rained."

Since ようだ involves the speaker's reasoning process, it is not compatible with a phrase identifying the source of information.

×テレビのニュースによると、雨が降るようだ。

(*intended*: "According to the news on TV, it appears that it will rain.")

However, ようだ is often used with the adverb どうやら "seemingly, as I surmise," which indicates that the speaker has taken time to consider the situation.

どうやら雨が降ったようだ。

"(Seemingly,) it appears to have rained."

The colloquial counterpart of ようだ, みたいだ, generally attaches to a plain form. However, the だ form of the copula is dropped before みたいだ.

Conjugation patterns with みたいだ

Plain-style verb	雨が降る "it rains" 雨が降らない 雨が降った 雨が降らなかった	[plain] みたいだ みたいじゃない みたいだった みたいじゃなかった
い-adjective	暑い "(it) is hot" 暑くない 暑かった 暑くなかった	
な-adjective	さわやか**だ** "(it) is refreshing" さわやかじゃない さわやかだった さわやかじゃなかった	[polite] みたいです みたいじゃありません (or みたいじゃないです) みたいでした みたいじゃありませんでした

Noun	晴れ**だ** "(it) is a sunny day" 晴れじゃない 晴れだった 晴れじゃなかった	(or みたいじゃなかったです)

Here are some example sentences:

今週末、台風が来る**みたい**よ。
"It seems like a typhoon will come this weekend."

田中さんが沖縄にいる間、ずっと雨だった**みたい**。
"It seems like it was raining for the entire time while Mr. Tanaka was in Okinawa."

Grammatical discussions of ようだ and みたいだ often contrast them with a similar (but slightly different) form, らしい, which also expresses the speaker's inference. The difference is that, in the case of らしい, the information on which the speaker bases his/her conjecture is mediated by others. For this reason, らしい may be used with a source phrase.

テレビのニュースによると、雨が降るらしい。
"According to the news on TV, it looks like it will rain."

Like みたいだ, らしい generally attaches to a plain form. However, だ is again dropped. Although it conjugates as an い-adjective, the negative forms are not used in practice.

Conjugation patterns with らしい

Plain-style verb	雨が降る "it rains" 雨が降らない 雨が降った 雨が降らなかった	[plain] らしい らしかった
い-adjective	暑い "(it) is hot" 暑くない 暑かった 暑くなかった	[polite] らしいです らしかったです

な-adjective	さわやか**だ** "(it) is refreshing" さわやかじゃない さわやかだった さわやかじゃなかった	[plain] らしい らしかった
Noun	晴れ**だ** "(it) is a sunny day" 晴れじゃない 晴れだった 晴れじゃなかった	[polite] らしいです らしかったです

See Unit 16 for a related expression for hearsay, そうだ₂.

Presumption: [P-plain^(no/na)] はずだ

はずだ "It is supposed to be the case that … /As far as I know …" is used to express what the speaker believes to be true on the basis of some reliable information or established knowledge.

夕焼けがきれいだから、明日は晴れる**はずだ**。

"Since the sunset is beautiful, it will be sunny tomorrow."

The adverb たしか "if I recall correctly" is often used with はずだ after the speaker verifies the likelihood of the event against his/her memory.

たしか昨日の最高気温は8度だった**はずだ**。

"If I recall correctly, the highest temperature yesterday was 8 °C."

The following table summarizes the conjugation patterns with はずだ:

Conjugation patterns with はずだ

Plain-style verb	雨が降る "it rains" 雨が降らない 雨が降った 雨が降らなかった	[plain] はずだ はずじゃない はずだった はずじゃなかった
い-adjective	暑い "(it) is hot" 暑くない 暑かった 暑くなかった	

な-adjective	さわやか**な** "(it) is refreshing" さわやかじゃない さわやかだった さわやかじゃなかった	[polite] はずです はずじゃありません (or はずじゃないです) はずでした はずじゃありませんでした (or はずじゃなかったです)
Noun	晴れの "(it) is a sunny day" 晴れじゃない 晴れだった 晴れじゃなかった	

The forms before はずだ follow noun-modifying patterns. A past form is used in this context when the speaker believes that something has already happened.

このあたりには何度も 雷 が落ちたはずだ。
"As far as I know, lightning struck this area many times."

If you use はずだった, you can indicate or imply that something that was supposed to happen, or to have happened, did not happen.

昨日は大阪で雷雨になる**はずだった**。
"There was supposed to be a thunderstorm in Osaka yesterday."

雨戸を閉めた**はずだった**のに。
"I thought I had closed the rain shutter."

Unlike the English expression "be supposed to," this pattern cannot be used for events that the subject feels committed to. Use ことになっている "it has been arranged/agreed that ..." in such cases. (*See* Unit 14 for the explanation of ことになる "be decided that ...")

晴れたら行くことになっている。
"I am supposed to go if it gets sunny."

Exercise 15.1

Fill in the blanks with the most appropriate adverb from もしかしたら, たぶん, きっと, どうやら, and たしか. You can check the meaning of each sentence in the Key to exercises.

1. 空に真っ黒な雲が広がっている。(　　　　　) 雨が降るらしい。

2. 自信を持って頑張って下さい。(　　　　　) うまくいきますよ。

3. (　　　　　) 横山さんの出身は、神戸のはずですよね。

4. はっきりとは申し上げられませんが、(　　　　　) 明日までに出来るでしょう。

5. (　　　　　) 吉田さんは来ないかもしれません。

6. (　　　　　) 私の予想は間違っていたようですね。

Exercise 15.2

Choose the appropriate option. You can check the meaning of each sentence in the Key to exercises.

1. 明日は雨{だ/な/の/∅}でしょう。

2. あさっては雪{だ/な/の/∅}かもしれません。

3. 午前中は雷雨{だ/な/の/∅}はずです。

4. 午後は曇り{だ/な/の/∅}ようです。

5. 週末はいい天気{だ/な/の/∅}らしいです。

6. 来週いっぱいは晴れ{だ/な/の/∅}みたいです。

Exercise 15.3

Choose the appropriate option. You can check the meaning of each sentence in the Key to exercises.

1. 蔵本さんの結婚式は豪華{だ/な/の/∅}でしょう。

2. その話はヨーロッパでは有名{だ/な/の/∅}かもしれません。

3. 土曜日は暇{だ/な/の/∅}はずです。
4. ジョーンズさんはお寿司が好き{だ/な/の/∅}ようです。
5. 藤村先生はお元気{だ/な/の/∅}らしいです。
6. １５０万円は必要{だ/な/の/∅}みたいです。

Exercise 15.4

Change the predicate in the parentheses into the appropriate form. You can check the meaning of each sentence in the Key to exercises.

1. 明日は大雪に(なります)でしょう。
2. 今晩は(会議です)かもしれません。
3. この辺は、夜も(静かです)だろうね。
4. わあ、このケーキ、(おいしいです)そうですね。
5. 昨晩は、渋滞で(大変でした)でしょう。
6. 最近、ずいぶんテレビが安く(買えます)ようですね。
7. 悪いけど、明日は大学に(来られません)しれない。
8. 岸田さんは、大学に(受かりませんでした)らしいですよ。

Exercise 15.5

Following the example, combine each of the rationales from 1–4 with the appropriate conclusion from a–d and translate the completed sentence.

Example

田中さんは医者です / 頭がいいです
→ 田中さんは医者だから、頭がいい**はずです**。
"Because Ms. Tanaka is a doctor, I expect her to be intelligent."

1. キムさんは学生です
2. ユーさんの専攻は日本語です
3. ハリケーンが来ます
4. 高橋さんはテニスクラブのメンバーです

a. 日本語がよく分かります
b. あまりお金がありません
c. テニスが上手です
d. 明日は大雨です

Exercise 15.6

Suppose that you had a bad day with things not turning out in the way you had expected. Following the example, describe what you had expected and what actually happened.

Example

You were supposed to wake up at 6 a.m., but you could not.

午前6時に起きるはずだったんですが、起きられませんでした。

1. You were supposed to go to an 8 o'clock class, but you could not.

2. You were supposed to finish the homework, but you did not have the time.

3. You were supposed to meet your friend at 1 p.m., but she did not come until 1:45 p.m.

4. You were supposed to play tennis, but it rained.

5. You were supposed to have a date (デートをする), but your date (デートの相手) did not come.

Exercise 15.7

Change the following sentences into conjectures based on intuitive judgment by attaching そうだ and making appropriate adjustments to their endings. For those sentences to which そうだ cannot be applied, use ようだ to express speaker's inferences. You can check the meaning of each completed sentence in the Key to exercises.

1. あの先生は厳しい。

2. この映画はおもしろくない。

3. あの人は学生だ。

4. 土曜日は無理だ。

5. アラスカの夏は暑くない。

6. 昨日は、雨が降らなかった。

UNIT 16

Quotation

There are two different types of quotation: direct and indirect. A direct quote is an utterance that the speaker deems a verbatim reproduction of the original utterance. An indirect quote is a restatement of the original by the speaker. In English, a direct quote typically appears accompanied by quotation marks and an indirect quote by the word "that."

DIRECT QUOTATION:	John said, **"I will be there soon."**
INDIRECT QUOTATION:	John said **that he would be there soon**.

Notice that the two types are distinguished not only by the presence of quotation marks or the word "that" but also by the differences in the use of personal pronouns, tensed forms, and time and place expressions inside the quotation.

In this unit, we study how the same type of distinction is made in Japanese.

Direct quotation

To quote an utterance of someone verbatim, use the following pattern:

Direct quotation

Agent = Subj./ topic	Addressee	Direct quote	Part.	V
先生は	私に	「明日はテストです。」	と	おっしゃった。
The teacher said to me "There will be a test tomorrow."				

Direct quotation in Japanese employs the **QUOTATIVE PARTICLE** と. One basic function of と is to incorporate an extraneous element into a sentence to give a lively "on-the-scene" impression. For instance, と is used for incorporating noises and sounds into a sentence.

犬がワンとほえた。
"A dog barked, 'Ruff.'"

What people say can also be reported almost word-for-word by using と, be it a statement, a question, or a command.

In quoting a statement, the quotative particle is combined with the verb 言う "say," its honorific counterpart おっしゃる "say," and the humble counterparts 申す "say" and 申し上げる "tell," among others. The following shows an exchange in which a direct quote is elicited. Note that the polite form of おっしゃる is slightly irregular おっしゃいます:

A: 先生は何とおっしゃいましたか。
"What did the professor say?"
B: 先生は結果は明日まで分かりませんとおっしゃいました。
"The professor said, 'I won't have the results until tomorrow.'"

You may optionally mark a direct quote with the Japanese quotation marks called *kagikakko*.

先生は「結果は明日まで分かりません。」とおっしゃいました。
"The professor said, 'I won't have the results until tomorrow.'"

In left-to-right horizontal writing, an upper left bracket 「 marks the beginning of a quote, and a lower right bracket 」 its end. In vertical writing, a quote begins with the upper right bracket and closes with a lower left bracket.

「まだ分_わかりません。」

「まだ分_わかりません。」

Direct quotation of other sentence types parallels direct quotation of a statement. To quote a question, attach the quotative particle after the quoted question and use 言^いう "say." You can also use a verb for seeking information such as 聞^きく "ask" and 尋^{たず}ねる "inquire."

助手^{じょしゅ}は学生^{がくせい}に「実験^{じっけん}を始^{はじ}めようか」と {聞^ききました/尋^{たず}ねました}。
"The assistant asked the students, 'Shall we begin the experiment?'"

To quote a request, use 言^いう "say," 頼^{たの}む "request," or お願^{ねが}いする "(politely) request" after と.

教授^{きょうじゅ}は助手^{じょしゅ}に「温度^{おんど}を調^{しら}べて下^{くだ}さい」と {言^いいました/頼^{たの}みました}。
"The professor said to the assistant, 'Please check the temperature.'"

Indirect quotation

Whether quoting a statement, a question, or a request, Japanese indirect quotes retain the same tense as the corresponding direct quotes, unlike English indirect quotes. In general, an indirect quote's predicate must be in the plain style. References to temporal points and places as well as personal pronouns and the LEVEL OF SPEECH are adjusted from the main clause speaker's perspective.

Quoting a statement indirectly: [P-plain] と言う

To quote a statement indirectly, use the following pattern:

Indirect quotation

Agent = Subj./ topic	Addressee	Indirect quote (P-plain)	Part.	V
先生は	私に	翌日はテストだ	と	おっしゃった。
The teacher said that there would be a test on the following day.				

Compare the following two statements, the first with a direct quote and the second with an indirect quote:

先生は「結果は明日まで分かりません。」とおっしゃいました。
[direct]
"The professor said, 'I won't have the results until tomorrow.'"

先生は結果は翌日まで分からないとおっしゃいました。
[indirect]
"The professor said that he would not have the results until the following day."

The quotative particle と is employed in both statements, but the predicate of the indirect quote in the second must be in the plain style (i.e. 分からない instead of 分かりません). Although the tense of the indirect quote's predicate is identical to that of the corresponding direct quote, in the indirect quote relative references to temporal points and places are adjusted from the main clause speaker's perspective as deemed necessary (i.e. 翌日 "the following day" instead of 明日 "tomorrow").

Conversation particles such as ね and よ, which can appear in direct quotes, are excluded from indirect quotes, as shown below:

橋本さんは「実験は成功でしたよ。」と言った。 [direct]
"Mr. Hashimoto said, 'The experiment was a success.'"

橋本さんは実験は成功だったと言った。 [indirect]
"Mr. Hashimoto said that the experiment was a success."

Personal pronouns and the level of speech are also adjusted from the perspective of the main-clause speaker. Below, a professor quotes a student's utterance directly in the first and indirectly in the second. In the indirect quote, the pronoun 私 "I" and the unmarked plain verb form 来る "come" appear, replacing the direct quote's honorific title 先生 "professor" and the humble polite verb 伺います "pay a visit."

その学生は「先生の研究室に伺います。」と言った。[direct]
"The student said 'I will come to your office, Professor.'"

その学生は私の研究室に来ると言った。[indirect]
"The student said that he would come to my office."

The main verb 言う "say" often appears as 言っている, a [V-て] いる form (*see* Units 2 and 8). Unlike 言う, which draws the listener's attention to the fact that someone said something, 言っている with an indirect quote draws the attention to the continuity and hence the currency of the claim. Consequently, it is often used to convey a message.

清水さんは実験は失敗かもしれないと言っていました。
"Mr. Shimizu was saying that the experiment might fail."

The quotative function of と is extended to the function of marking information that is not fully established; in other words, what the subject believes, has heard, has just realized, and so on. Therefore, it is also compatible with verbs such as 思う "think," 聞く "hear," and 分かる "realize."

うまく行くと思います。
"I think it will go well."

実験が成功したと聞きました。
"I heard that the experiment succeeded."

成功のニュースは誤報だったと分かった。
"We learned that news of the success was false."

Quoting a question indirectly: [P-plain] か(と)聞く

To quote a question indirectly, use the following pattern:

Indirect question

Agent = Subj./ topic	Addressee	Indirect quote (P-plain^(da-drop))	Part.	V
刑事_{けいじ}は	私_{わたし}に	裏_{うら}の窓_{まど}をしめた	か(と)	聞_きいた。
The detective asked me if I closed the back window.				

The indirect quotation of questions shares most of the characteristics of the indirect quotation of statements. In order to quote a question indirectly, formulate plain-style counterparts of polite-style questions in the following manner:

[verb-ending]
裏_{うら}の窓_{まど}を閉_しめましたか   → 裏_{うら}の窓_{まど}を閉_しめたか
"Did you close the back window?"

[い-adjective-ending]
合鍵_{あいかぎ}はないですか   → 合鍵_{あいかぎ}はないか
"Aren't there any duplicate keys?"

[copula-ending]
鍵_{かぎ}を持_もっているのは誰_{だれ}ですか → 鍵_{かぎ}を持_もっているのは誰_{だれ}か
"Who is the one that has a key?"

If the question ends with a verb or an い-adjective, just insert its plain-style variant before the quotative particle. You can optionally drop と.

刑事_{けいじ}は裏_{うら}の窓_{まど}をしめたか(と)聞_きいた。
"The detective asked me if I closed the back window."

刑事_{けいじ}は合鍵_{あいかぎ}はないか(と)聞_きいた。
"The detective asked me if I had any duplicate keys."

And if you drop と when quoting a yes-no question, you can optionally insert どうか "(whether) or not" in the following manner:

刑事は裏の窓をしめたかどうか聞いた。
"The detective asked me whether or not I closed the back window."

刑事は合鍵があるかどうか聞いた。
"The detective asked me whether or not I had any duplicate keys."

Questions that end with the copula exhibit slightly more complex characteristics. That is, if the quotative particle is retained, you must drop だ just as when quoting a plain question verbatim (*see also* Unit 7).

刑事は鍵を持っているのは誰かと聞いた。
"The detective asked me who had a key."

On the other hand, if と is dropped, だ is optionally retained.

刑事は鍵を持っているのは誰(だ)か聞いた。
"The detective asked me who had a key."

The question particle か means that the subject is trying to assess the information. Hence, this pattern is compatible with verbs related to such processes as asking, pondering, answering, having the answer to, avoiding, and failing to answer a question.

何時だったか聞いた。　　"I asked her what time it was."
どこにいたか知っている。　"I know where s/he was."
誰(だ)か言わなかった。　　"I did not tell them who it was."
最後にいつ見たか忘れた。　"I forgot when I saw it last."

Many verbs that can appear with か can also appear with と.

何時か分かった。　　　　　午前3時だったと分かった。
"I found out what time it was."　"I found out that it was 3 a.m."

どうするか決めた。　　　　やると決めた。
"I made up my mind what to do."　"I made up my mind to do it."

Some verbs such as 聞く and 考える have different meanings depending on the particle.

行くか聞いた。
"I asked if they would go."

行くと聞いた。
"I heard that they were going."

出来るか考えた。
"I wondered if it was possible."

出来ると考えた。
"I concluded that it was possible."

However, 思う "think," unlike 考える above, cannot appear with か because it does not have the sense of deliberation.

出来ると思った。
"I thought/felt it was possible."

Quoting an instruction indirectly: [volitional V-plain non-past] ように言う

To quote an instruction indirectly, use the following pattern.

Indirect question

Agent = Subj./ topic	Addressee	Action to be taken (volitional V-plain non-past)		V
店員は	客に	明日もう一度電話する	ように	言った。
The store clerk told the customer to call them again tomorrow.				

Indirect quotation of instructions also shares most of the characteristics of indirect quotation of statements. The difference is that the former requires a non-past volitional verb followed by ように, which we studied in the sense of "so that" in Unit 13.

店員は客に明日もう一度電話するように言った。
"The store clerk told the customer to call them again tomorrow."

医者は患者に薬を飲むように言った。
"The doctor told the patient to take the medicine."

母は弟に起きるように言った。
"My mother told my younger brother to wake up."

警部は巡査について来るように言った。
"The police captain told the patrolman to follow him."

These indirect quotes neutralize the differences in nuance that are present in the corresponding direct quotes below:

Polite request

店員は客に「明日もう一度電話してくださいませんか。」と言った。

"The store clerk said to the customer, 'Could you call us again tomorrow?'"

Request

医者は患者に「薬を飲んで下さい。」と言った。

"The doctor said to the patient, 'Please take the medicine.'"

Motherly command

母は弟に「起きなさい。」と言った。

"My mother said to my younger brother, 'Wake up.'"

Command

警部は巡査に「ついて来い。」と言った。

"The police captain said to the patrolman, 'Follow me!'"

In order to reproduce the nuances of direct quotes in indirect quotes, you can use different main verbs.

店員は客に明日もう一度電話するように頼んだ。

"The store clerk asked the customer to call them again tomorrow."

医者は患者に薬を飲むように指示した。

"The doctor instructed the patient to take the medicine."

母は弟に起きるように言った。

"My mother told my younger brother to wake up."

警部は巡査について来るように命令した。

"The police captain ordered the patrolman to follow him."

The last three examples, which contain relatively brusque requests, can also be rephrased using the command pattern explained in Unit 10.

医者は患者に薬を飲めと指示した。
"The doctor instructed the patient to take the medicine."

母は弟に起きろと言った。
"My mother told my younger brother to wake up."

警部は巡査について来いと命令した。
"The police captain ordered the patrolman to follow him."

Quotation patterns with verbs of emotion

The quotative particleと may be followed by a verb meaning an emotive reaction, such as 怒る "get angry," がっかりする "be disappointed," 笑う "laugh," and 喜ぶ "rejoice." In such cases, the sentences mean that the quoted part was uttered or felt with a corresponding emotion.

教授はちゃんと結果を確認しろと怒った。
"The professor angrily told them to verify the results properly."

助手は失敗だったとがっかりした。
"The assistant was disappointed believing that it had failed."

学生はもう一度やろうと笑った。
"The students cheerfully suggested that they should try it again."

Other uses of the quotation pattern

Many useful expressions take advantage of the function of と to highlight non-established or unfamiliar information. For instance, you can use the verb 言う to introduce yourself. Its humble equivalent, 申す, is used for added formality.

池田と言います/と申します。
"I am called Ikeda." (= My name is Ikeda.)

You can use the pattern 「〜」というN to cite a name unfamiliar to you or (presumably) new to the listener.

さっき「松本さん」という人から電話がありましたよ。
"A little earlier there was a call from a person identifying himself as Mr. Matsumoto."

朝ご飯に「ブリヌイ」というロシアのパンケーキを食べました。
"I ate a Russian pancake called *blini* for breakfast."

「与作」という店を知っていますか。
"Do you know a shop called *Yosaku*?"

昨日「トリトン」というレストランへ行きました。
"Yesterday, I went to a restaurant called *Toriton*."

The expression 「〜」というの "the one that is called ..." is useful for referring to an unfamiliar thing whose identity you cannot determine.

「うめぼし」というのはすっぱいですねぇ。
"The thing called *umeboshi* is sour, isn't it?"

Using this expression and the ending ことだ "be equivalent to," you can give the formal definition of a word. Here, こと is the abstract noun こと (*see BJ* Unit 11):

「パソコン」というのは、パーソナル・コンピューターのことです。
"The word *pasokon* refers to 'personal computers.'"

「花見」というのは桜の花を見ることです。
"The word *hanami* refers to the event of watching cherry blossoms."

This combination often appears in an exchange for clarification of an unfamiliar term.

A: 「パソコン」というのは何(のこと)ですか。
　　"What is *pasokon*?"

B: パーソナル・コンピュータのことですよ。
　　"It means 'personal computer.'"

In colloquial speech, というのは is often contracted to って.

> A: 「パソコン」って<ruby>何<rt>なん</rt></ruby>(のこと)ですか。
> "What is *pasokon*?"

> B: パーソナル・コンピュータのことですよ。
> "It means 'personal computer.'"

Hearsay: [P-plain] そうだ₂

The auxiliary ending そうだ₂, attached to a plain direct form, is used to report something that you heard or read, without vouching for its truthfulness.

Hearsay

P-plain	Auxiliary adjective
<ruby>手紙<rt>てがみ</rt></ruby>が<ruby>着<rt>つ</rt></ruby>いた	そうだ。
I heard that the letter arrived.	

This sentence is functionally similar to the earlier example with the verb <ruby>聞<rt>き</rt></ruby>く "hear":

> <ruby>手紙<rt>てがみ</rt></ruby>が<ruby>着<rt>つ</rt></ruby>いたと<ruby>聞<rt>き</rt></ruby>きました。
> "I heard that the letter arrived."

The difference is that そうだ₂ leaves unspecified the source of information or manner in which information was gathered. For example, the following sentence may be uttered regardless of whether you have heard of the accident from your friend, watched it on TV, or read about it in a newspaper:

> <ruby>事故<rt>じこ</rt></ruby>があったそうです。
> "Reportedly, there was an accident."

On the other hand, the following sentence may only be used if you have actually heard about it:

> <ruby>事故<rt>じこ</rt></ruby>があったと<ruby>聞<rt>き</rt></ruby>きました。
> "I heard that there was an accident."

Do not confuse the hearsay そうだ₂ with そうだ₁ discussed in Unit 15, which attaches to an adjectival or verbal stem to express a conjecture.

Hearsay

事故の確率が高いそうだ。

"I heard that the accident probability is high."

Conjecture

事故の確率が高そうだ。

"It looks like the accident probability is high."

If you want to specify the source when using そうだ₂, you can use [N] によると "according to," or [N] によれば "according to, if you believe." (*See* Unit 18 for explanations of と-clause and ば-clause.)

ニュースによると、南アメリカの鉱山で事故があったそうで
す。

"According to the news, there was an accident in a South American mine."

会社の説明によれば、死者はいなかったそうです。

"According to the company, there were no deaths."

Do not confuse a similar pattern [N] によって "depending on" with these expressions:

国によって、安全基準は違う。

"Depending on the country, the safety standards are different."

See Unit 15 for a closely related expression らしい.

Exercise 16.1

Fill in the blanks with the appropriate particle. You can check the meaning of each sentence in the Key to exercises.

1. 橋本さんは4時までに来る(　　)言っていました。
2. 先生がどちらにいらっしゃる(　　)分かりますか。

3. コンサートは9時ごろからだ( ) 思_{おも}います。

3. コンサートは9時_じごろからだ( ) 思_{おも}います。

4. 鍵_{かぎ}をどこに置_おいた( ) 忘_{わす}れました。

5. 山崎_{やまさき}( ) 申_{もう}します。よろしくお願_{ねが}いします。

Exercise 16.2

Rewrite the following sentences using appropriate indirect quotes. You can check the meaning of each sentence in the Key to exercises.

1. 池田_{いけだ}さんは「阿部_{あべ}さんは車_{くるま}がありませんよ。」と言_いっていました。

2. ボブは「ハワイ旅行_{りょこう}は楽_{たの}しかったです。」と言_いったらしい。

3. 道子_{みちこ}は「おいしいラーメンが食_たべたいなぁ。」と言_いっていた。

4. リーさんは「インタビューはいつでしたか。」と尋_{たず}ねました。

5. シモナさんは「私_{わたし}の母_{はは}はロシア人_{じん}です。」と言_いいました。

6. 先生_{せんせい}は「僕_{ぼく}の父_{ちち}はパリにいます。」とおっしゃいました。

7. 井上_{いのうえ}さんに「お母_{かあ}さんはお元気_{げんき}ですか。」と聞_きかれました。

8. 私_{わたし}は姉_{あね}に「あなたは小_{ちい}さい時_{とき}よく近所_{きんじょ}の子供_{こども}とけんかをしたのよ。」と言_いわれました。

Exercise 16.3

Insert の in the parentheses if necessary. Insert Ø otherwise. You can check the meaning of each sentence in the Key to exercises.

1. A: 昨日_{きのう}、「カフェ・タージ」という( )インド料理_{りょうり}のレストランに行ったんですが、あそこのナンはおいしかったです。

   B: その「ナン」という( )は何_{なん}ですか。

2. A: インドのパンですよ。

   B: ああ、あのうすいパン( )ことですね。それで、その「カフェ・タージ」という( )はどこにあるんですか。

3. A: 新宿_{しんじゅく}ですよ。地下鉄_{ちかてつ}の駅_{えき}を出_でてすぐの「ミ・アモーレ」
    という(　　)ビルの3階_{さんがい}です。

Exercise 16.4

Suppose you hear the following unfamiliar words while watching a
Japanese TV program at your host family's home. Formulate questions
for asking what they are. Then choose the likely answer for each item
from a to d below. You can check the meaning of each dialogue in the
Key to exercises.

1. お花見_{はなみ}

2. ホッチキス

3. パリコレ

4. 魔法瓶_{まほうびん}

a. magic bottle の意味_{いみ}で、飲_のみ物_{もの}を保温_{ほおん}できる入_いれ物_{もの}のことです
   よ。

b. 英語_{えいご}では、stapler と言_いいます。日本語_{にほんご}では、作_{つく}った人_{ひと}の名前_{なまえ}を
   とったんですよ。

c. 桜_{さくら}の花_{はな}を見_みに行_いくことですよ。ほかの花_{はな}ではこう言_いわないん
   です。

d. パリ・コレクションのことです。カー・ナビゲーションからの
   カーナビとか、日本語_{にほんご}にはこういう言葉_{ことば}がたくさんありますよ。

UNIT 17

Describing notable experiences

Main target grammar in this unit

<ruby>話<rt>はな</rt></ruby>したことがある、<ruby>話<rt>はな</rt></ruby>すことがある、<ruby>話<rt>はな</rt></ruby>してみる

"Have you ever been to Japan?" "Yes, twice." "When was the first time you went to Japan?" Such an exchange about notable experiences is likely to take place, for example, during an interview. In this unit, we will study some ways in which notable experiences are described.

First-time experience: はじめて

To indicate that someone is doing or did something for the first time, you can use the adverb はじめて "for the first time."

<ruby>１７才<rt>じゅうななさい</rt></ruby>の<ruby>時<rt>とき</rt></ruby>にはじめて<ruby>1人<rt>ひとり</rt></ruby>で<ruby>旅行<rt>りょこう</rt></ruby>しました。
"I traveled alone for the first time when I was seventeen."

<ruby>僕<rt>ぼく</rt></ruby>の<ruby>お母<rt>かあ</rt></ruby>さんは、1985<ruby>年<rt>ねん</rt></ruby>にはじめてパソコンを<ruby>使<rt>つか</rt></ruby>ったんだって。
"I heard my mom used a personal computer for the first time in 1985."

To emphasize the date when something happened for the first time, you can use the focus pattern [P-plain$^{(na)}$] のは〜だ, which we studied in *BJ* Unit 11.

ファストフードチェーンがはじめて<ruby>日本<rt>にほん</rt></ruby>で<ruby>店<rt>みせ</rt></ruby>を<ruby>開<rt>ひら</rt></ruby>いたのは、1971<ruby>年<rt>ねん</rt></ruby>だった。
"It was 1971 when a fast-food chain opened a store in Japan for the first time."

アメリカの会社<ruby>会社<rt>かいしゃ</rt></ruby>がはじめてオンラインで本<ruby>本<rt>ほん</rt></ruby>を売<ruby>売<rt>う</rt></ruby>ったのは、1994年<ruby>年<rt>ねん</rt></ruby>でした。

"It was 1994 when a US company sold books online for the first time."

Do not confuse はじめて with はじめに "first/in the beginning/at the onset," which is used in the following manner:

この会社<ruby>会社<rt>かいしゃ</rt></ruby>は、**はじめに**本<ruby>本<rt>ほん</rt></ruby>を売<ruby>売<rt>う</rt></ruby>って、次<ruby>次<rt>つぎ</rt></ruby>にコンピューターを売<ruby>売<rt>う</rt></ruby>った。

"This company sold books first and computers next."

Unique past experiences: [P-plain^(no/na) past]
ことがある

Even though many first-time experiences eventually become routines or are forgotten, some experiences remain unique and noteworthy. To proudly announce or secretly confide such past experiences, use the pattern [P-plain^(no/na) past] ことがある, as in the following:

海外<ruby>海外<rt>かいがい</rt></ruby>で働<ruby>働<rt>はたら</rt></ruby>いたことがあります。

"I have the experience of having worked overseas."

This pattern literally means "have the experience of having done something." The preceding verb must be in the plain style because こと is the abstract nominalizer (*see BJ* Unit 11) and is in the past tense because the event is a past event. The non-past tense form ある or あります indicates the experience up to the present time.

Here are some more example sentences:

あの人<ruby>人<rt>ひと</rt></ruby>、どこかで会<ruby>会<rt>あ</rt></ruby>ったことがあるなあ。

"I've met her somewhere (but I cannot remember where)."

彼氏<ruby>彼氏<rt>かれし</rt></ruby>の携帯<ruby>携帯<rt>けいたい</rt></ruby>をこっそり見<ruby>見<rt>み</rt></ruby>たことがある?

"Have you ever checked your boyfriend's cell phone secretly?"

今<ruby>今<rt>いま</rt></ruby>の会社<ruby>会社<rt>かいしゃ</rt></ruby>をやめようと思<ruby>思<rt>おも</rt></ruby>ったことが何度<ruby>何度<rt>なんど</rt></ruby>もあります。

"I have considered quitting my current company many times."

If you had experienced something prior to a certain point in the past, use the past tense form あった or ありました.

それまでに2度会ったことがありました。
"I had met her twice up to that point."

If on some rare occasions you missed a regular activity, you can indicate it by using a negative form before こと.

大雪で家の外に1週間も出られなかったことがあります。
"There was a time when I could not get out of the house for a week due to heavy snow."

The above pattern, ～なかったことがある, characterizes the experience of occasionally missing something in the past as notable. On the other hand, if you use an affirmative form before and a negative ending after こと, you can indicate either the lack of a notable experience or a unique situation of never having had a certain experience.

外国で働いたことはありません。
"I have never worked in a foreign country."

そんなこと聞いたことがないよ。
"I have never heard such a thing."

佐藤先生は、ファストフードレストランで食べたことがないんだそうです。めずらしいですね。
"Professor Sato has never eaten at a fast-food restaurant. That's rare, isn't it?"

あの課長は部下と飲みに行ったことが1度もないんだって。
"They say that that section chief has never been to have a drink with his junior employees."

Notable on-going experience: [P-plain^(no/na) non-past] ことがある

Certain recurrent and on-going experiences may also be considered as notable and worth mentioning. To describe such experiences, use a non-past verb with ことがある.

今でもまだ友だちに手紙を書くことがあります。
"Even now there are still times when I write letters to my friends."

時々仕事で日本に行くことがあります。
"I sometimes have the opportunity to go to Japan on business."

If doing something is a norm and you sometimes fail to do so, you can indicate it by using a negative form before こと.

コーヒーを飲みすぎて寝られないことがたまにあります。
"Occasionally I cannot fall asleep having drunk too much coffee."

If the form before こと is affirmative and the sentence ends in ない/ありません, the total sentence describes an absence of a certain custom.

インドでは、左手で食べることはない。
"In India, people do not eat with their left hand."

Casual adventures: [volitional V-て] みる

When you go to a foreign country, you will be introduced to new customs, food, products, etc., and will be required to be a little adventurous. Or when you encounter some minor problem, ideally you will come up with a quick fix using available resources. Japanese has a construction that expresses such adventurous or resourceful attitudes: the て-form of a verb followed by みる. This construction literally means "do something and see." Therefore when you use this construction you should expect to be able to verify the outcome of the action relatively quickly, as in the following situations:

デパートの食品売り場でいろいろ日本の食べ物を食べてみました。おいしかったです。
"I tried various Japanese foods at the food section of a department store. They were delicious."

気分がよくなると聞いたので、しょうがを少しかじってみた。
"I nibbled on a little ginger because I heard that I would feel better (if I did)."

177

日本人と友だちになりたかったので、大学のクラブに入って
みた。

"Because I wanted to become friends with Japanese individuals,
I joined a university student organization."

You can invite someone to do something new in the following manner:

一口食べてみませんか。

"How about having a bite?"

ちょっと使ってみたらどうですか。

"Why don't you give it a try?"

Exercise 17.1

Choose between はじめに "in the beginning" and はじめて "for the first
time." You can check the meaning of each sentence in the Key to
exercises.

1. 自分では気がつかなかったんですけど、さっき言われて{はじ
   めに/はじめて}あのポスターに気がつきました。

2. では、テストを始めます。{はじめに/はじめて}名前を書いてく
   ださい。

3. {はじめに/はじめて}私が風邪をひいて、それから家族みんな
   が風邪をひきました。

4. {はじめに/はじめて}日本に行ったのはいつですか。

Exercise 17.2

Based on your knowledge of world history and the historical timeline in
the box, decide whether or not each of the following statements is true.
You can check the meaning of each sentence in the Key to exercises.

781	First recorded eruption of Mount Fuji.
1543	The Portuguese introduce firearms to Japanese. Shortly afterward, Japanese warlords begin to use firearms in warfare.
1707	Last eruption of Mount Fuji.

> 1792　The Russians attempt to establish trade relations
> 　　　　with Japan.
> 1854　Commodore Perry forces the Japanese government
> 　　　　to reopen Japan to the West.

1.　[True / False]　　＿＿＿＿
　　１６世紀になるまで、日本人は銃を作ったことがなかった。

2.　[True / False]　　＿＿＿＿
　　ペリーが日本に来るまで、ヨーロッパ人は、日本に来たことが
　　なかった。

3.　[True / False]　　＿＿＿＿
　　富士山は噴火したことがあるが、この３００年間は噴火したこ
　　とがない。

4.　[True / False]　　＿＿＿＿
　　人間は月に行ったことがない。

Exercise 17.3

Following the example, construct questions that will elicit the answers.
You can check the meaning of each dialog in the Key to exercises.

Example

　　A: 友だちに**カードを書くことがありますか**。

　　　"Do you ever write a card to a friend?"

　　B: ええ、時々書きますよ。

　　　"Yes, I sometimes do."

1.　A: 渡辺さんに＿＿＿＿＿＿＿＿。
　　B: ええ、たまに会いますよ。

2.　A: 今でも辞書を＿＿＿＿＿＿＿＿。
　　B: いいえ、ぜんぜん使いません。

3. A: オンラインショッピングを＿＿＿＿＿。

   B: ええ、よくしますよ。

4. A: 映画館で＿＿＿＿＿。

   B: ええ、時々見ます。

Exercise 17.4

Mr. Maeda has been living alone in a remote jungle without any human contact for the past 30 years. Continue the following passage with a description of three technological gadgets that he has not seen or has not used. You can check the meaning of the completed sample passage in the Key to exercises.

前田さんは、この30年間ジャングルから出たことがない。
ジャングルで手に入るもので小屋を作って1人で生活している。
動物たちはたくさん見るが、人に会ったことは一度もないし、
手紙を書いたことも受け取ったこともない。もちろん＿＿＿＿＿

＿＿＿＿＿＿＿＿＿＿。

Exercise 17.5

Change the verb in the parentheses into the appropriate form. You can check the meaning of the passage in the Key to exercises.

リーさんは、今、横浜でホームステイをしている。リーさんは、今日はじめて、東京のデパートに1人で(行く)みた。デパートの1階で靴を何足か(はく)みてから、6階の電気屋に行って一番新しいタイプのノートパソコンを(試す)みた。2時ごろになっておなかがすいたので、8階の食堂に行って日本語で寿司とうどんを(注文する)みた。帰りにリーさんは、地下の食品売り場で店員が「お客さん、ちょっとこのお酒、(飲む)みませんか。」とか「一口(召し上がる)みてください。」とか言っているのを聞いた。

UNIT 18

Stipulating conditions

On many occasions an action, decision, or judgment depends on a prior condition. For instance, you may buy ten more lottery tickets **if you win one**. Or perhaps you decide not to buy any more tickets **once you win $100**. Or watching a news report of someone having bought a lucky ticket at one of your neighborhood stores, you might think, "**Had I bought a ticket there**, I could have turned into a millionaire." The bold parts of these examples are **CONDITIONAL CLAUSES**. In this unit, we will study different types of conditional clauses and their usage in Japanese.

Conditional clauses versus embedded questions

In English, a conditional clause commonly starts with "if," although not all clauses that begin with "if" are conditional clauses. That is, there are two types of *if*-clauses: embedded questions and conditional clauses.

I don't know **if I have enough cash**. [embedded question]

I will be in trouble **if I don't have enough cash**. [conditional clause]

The two types of *if*-clauses share the sense of uncertainty. However, the first type is actually a yes-no question and can be rephrased in the following manner:

I don't know **whether (or not) I have enough cash**.

181

We studied the Japanese counterpart of this pattern in the discussion of indirect quotation in Unit 16.

お金が足りるか分からない。
"I don't know if I have enough money."

The second type of *if*-clause differs from the above in that it stands for a **HYPOTHETICAL CONDITION** leading to a consequence and can be moved to the beginning of the sentence.

If I don't have enough cash, I will be in trouble.

The Japanese language sharply distinguishes between embedded questions and conditional clauses. We will study the conditional clauses in this unit.

Three types of conditionals in Japanese

The last English conditional sentence above can be translated into Japanese in three different ways.

現金が足りなかったら、困るだろう。 [たら-clause]
"If I don't have enough cash, I will be in trouble."

現金が足りなければ、困るだろう。 [ば-clause]
"If I don't have enough cash, I will be in trouble."

現金が足りないと、困るだろう。 [と-clause]
"If I don't have enough cash, I will be in trouble."

The たら-clause, ば-clause, and と-clause are types of conditional clauses. These conditional clauses, unlike English *if*-clauses, must always precede the main clause following the general placement pattern of sentence-modifying clauses in Japanese (*see BJ* Unit 4).

Although the uses of たら-, ば-, and と-clauses may sometimes overlap, each type has its own characteristics that will make it suitable in some cases but not in others. In the following, we will study each of them carefully.

たら-clause

The たら-clause roughly translates into "if or when some condition is met, then …" The たら-part is formed by attaching ら to the **plain past form** of a predicate. Therefore, it sometimes appears as だら (e.g. 読んだら "if I/you/she/he read(s)").

Verbs

見る	→ 見たら	来る	→ 来たら
"see"	"if (I) see"	"come"	"if (I) come"

読む	→ 読んだら	する	→ したら
"read"	"if (I) read"	"do"	"if (I) do it"

い-adjectives and adjectival endings

安い	→ 安かったら	高い	→ 高かったら
"cheap"	"if (it) is cheap"	"expensive"	"if (it) is expensive"

買いたい	→ 買いたかったら	買わない	→ 買わなかったら
"want to buy"	"if (I) want to buy"	"not buy"	"if (I) don't buy"

な-adjectives and nouns

便利な	→ 便利だったら	あなた(だ)	→ あなただったら
"convenient"	"if it's convenient"	"(it is) you"	"if it's you"

In a manner similar to English *if*-clauses, the たら-clause can express hypothetical conditions.

宝くじに当たったら、お金を寄付します。
"If I win the lottery, I will donate the money."

クレジットカードを使ったら、手数料がかかります。
"If you use a credit card, there will be a service charge."

The たら-clause can express either a one-time hypothetical condition (as in the lottery example) or a recurring/habitual hypothetical condition (as in the credit card example). The adverb もし, often translated into English as "if," may optionally be added to emphasize the hypothetical nature of a condition that leads to a one-time consequence.

もし宝くじに当たったら、お金を全部寄付します。
"If I win the lottery by any chance, I will donate all the money."

The たら-clause interacts differently with an eventive and a stative predicate (*see* Unit 2). たら-clauses with stative predicates, as in the following, are always hypothetical.

安かったら、買います。
"If it is inexpensive, I will buy it."

買いたかったら、買って下さい。
"If you want to buy it, please buy it."

不良品だったら、お金を返してくれるそうです。
"If it's a defective product, they say they are going to return the money."

In addition to hypothetical conditions, たら-clauses with eventive predicates (*see* Unit 2) can also express less hypothetical conditions. For example, the たら-clause in the following sentence introduces a scheduled event as a condition and is better translated into English using "when."

今月の給料をもらったら、スーツを買うつもりです。
"When I get this month's salary, I plan to buy a suit."

Furthermore, the たら-clause with an eventive predicate expresses a FACTUAL CONDITION when the main predicate is in the past tense.

100ポンドを円に両替したら、13000円になりました。
"When I exchanged £100 to yen, it came to ¥13,000."

Note that the main event that follows a factual condition must be uncontrollable to the speaker in the sense that it is a surprising result, realization, or discovery.

× 両替したら、手数料を払いました。
(*intended*: "When I exchanged my money, I paid a service charge.")

o 両替したら、手数料がかかりました。
"When I exchanged my money, there was a service charge."

Since Japanese とき-clauses (*see BJ* Unit 12) are also translated into *when*-clauses, the たら-clause and とき-clause may appear interchangeable at times.

借金を全部返したら、また新しい車を買います。
"I will buy a new car again when/once I pay off the loan."

借金を全部返した時に、また新しい車を買います。
"I will buy a new car again (at the time) when I pay off the loan."

However, these patterns are not wholly equivalent. The たら-clause specifies the condition to be met for the main event to follow. This temporal organization of たら along with its meaning of uncertainty often brings out the sense of surprise or discovery, as is the case with the factual conditional use of the たら-clause. The とき-clause, by contrast, merely provides a temporal reference point at which time the main event takes place. Naturally, the uncontrollability requirement observed with the factual conditional use of the たら-clause does not apply to the とき-clause.

ドルに両替した時に、手数料を払いました。
"When I exchanged my money to dollars, I paid a service charge."

ば-clauses

The ば-clause means "if some condition holds, then ..." To make the ば-form of a verb, replace the last *u*-row syllable of its dictionary form with the corresponding *e*-row syllable and attach ば. This rule applies to derived (e.g. a potential form 買える "can buy") and complex verbs (e.g. し始める "start doing") as well. (*See* Appendix B for more examples.)

Verbs

見る	→	見れば	来る	→	来れば

見る → 見れば　　　来る → 来れば
"see"　　　"if (I) see"　　"come"　　"if (I) come"

読む → 読めば　　　する → すれば
"read"　　"if (I) read"　　"do"　　"if (I) do it"

買える → 買えれば　　し始める → し始めれば
"can buy"　"if (I) can buy"　"start doing"　"if (I) start
　　　　　　　　　　　　　　　　　　　doing"

To make the ば-form of an い-adjective, attach ければ to its stem form (i.e. dictionary form minus the last vowel い). This rule uniformly applies to all adjectival-endings including the plain-style negative forms of verbs.

い-adjectives and adjectival endings

安い → 安ければ　　　高い → 高ければ
"cheap"　　"if it is cheap"　"expensive"　"if it is
　　　　　　　　　　　　　　　　　　　expensive"

買いたい → 買いたければ　　買わない → 買わなけ
　　　　　　　　　　　　　　　　　　　　れば
"want to buy"　"if you want to buy"　"not buy"　"if you
　　　　　　　　　　　　　　　　　　　　don't buy"

Corresponding nominal forms are produced by attaching なら directly to a noun or to a な-adjectival stem. On initial inspection, they do not appear to be aligned with the verbal and adjectival types. However, なら is a shortened form of the older and more formal ならば, which shows a close affinity to the other ば-conditional forms.

な-adjectives and nouns

便利な → 便利なら(ば)　　あなた(だ) → あなた
　　　　　　　　　　　　　　　　　　　なら(ば)
"convenient"　"if it is　　　"(it is) you"　"if it is
　　　　　convenient"　　　　　　　　　you"

Many たら-clauses can be safely replaced by a ば-clause as shown below:

安ければ、買います。
"If it is cheap, I will buy it."

買いたければ、買って下さい。
"If you want to buy it, please buy it."

クレジットカードを使えば、手数料がかかります。
"If you use a credit card, there will be a service charge."

不良品なら、お金を返してくれるそうです。
"If it's a defective product, they say they are going to return the money."

However, its lack of tense marking (past or non-past) prevents the ば-clause from being used to express a factual condition for a single past event in the manner the たら-clause can be used.

× 100ドルを円に両替すれば、8000円になりました。
(*intended*: "If I exchanged $100 to yen, it came to ¥8,000.")

o 100ドルを円に両替したら、8000円になりました。
"When I exchanged $100 to yen, it came to ¥8,000."

This property does not prevent the ば-clause from being used to express a habitual or **COUNTERFACTUAL CONDITION** in the past (*see* the section on counterfactuals below).

あの頃は、100ドルを円に両替すれば、12000円になりました。
"In those days, if I exchanged $100 to yen, it came to ¥12,000."

クレジットカードを使えば、手続きが簡単だったのに。
"If you had used a credit card, the process would have been simpler."

Further constraints on ば-clauses

Above we said that many たら-clauses can be safely replaced by a ば-clause. However, whereas the main clause after a たら-clause tends to have a sense of new discovery or decision, the main clause after a ば-clause expresses a more matter-of-fact or controlled outcome. In this sense, ば-clauses are closer to English expressions introduced by "as long as" or "provided that" and are more effective as a means of conveying reassurance than たら-clauses.

今から貯金し始めれば、大丈夫ですよ。
"Provided you start saving now, you will be OK."

一生懸命 働けば、給料が上がりますよ。
"As long as you work hard, you will get a raise."

On the other hand, the sense of controlled connection constrains the use of ば-clauses in various other contexts. For one thing, a request for advice cannot appear after an eventive ば-clause. The たら-clause counterpart is perfectly acceptable.

× 給料が下がれば、どうしよう。
(*intended*: "If I get a pay reduction, what should I do?")

○ 給料が下がったら、どうしよう。
"If I get a pay reduction, what should I do?"

Nor can a request for action appear after a ば-clause expressing the addressee's action. The たら-clause counterpart is perfectly acceptable for this, too.

× 現金で払えば、レシートをもらって下さい。
(*intended*: "If you pay by cash, please ask for a receipt.")

○ 現金で払ったら、レシートをもらって下さい。
"If you pay by cash, please ask for a receipt."

A request with a ば-clause meaning an adverse condition for the addressee sounds too heartless or unconcerned. The たら-clause counterpart is again acceptable.

? 給料が下がれば、節約してください。
(*intended*: "If you get a pay reduction, please be thrifty.")

○ 給料が下がったら、節約してください。
"If you get a pay reduction, please be thrifty."

The combination of a ば-clause and a request is acceptable if the ば-clause is not under the control of the addressee or does not mean an adverse personal condition.

給料が上がれば、旅行でもしてください。
"If you get a raise, please travel."

ドルが下がれば、買って下さい。

"If the dollar becomes devalued, please buy dollars."

もしバイヤーが来れば、知らせてくれ。

"If a buyer comes, notify me."

と-clauses

The と-clause is formed by attaching と to the **plain non-past form** of the predicate.

Verbs

見る	→	見ると	来る	→	来ると
"see"		"if (I) see"	"come"		"if (I) come"

い-adjectives and adjectival endings

安い	→	安いと	買わない	→	買わないと
"cheap"		"if it's cheap"	"not buy"		"if (I) don't buy"

な-adjectives and nouns

便利な	→	便利だと	あなた(だ)	→	あなただと
"convenient"		"if it's convenient"	"(it is) you"		"if it's you"

Recall that a たら- or ば-clause can express either a one-time condition or a recurring/habitual condition. The と-clause crucially differs from them in that the condition-consequence sequence must be predetermined and recurring/habitual. Note that the first of the following sentences can be uttered only by a frequent shopper, and the second by a lucky individual who has won the lottery multiple times.

安いと、買います。

"Whenever something is inexpensive/discounted, I buy it."

宝くじに当たると、お金を寄付します。

"Whenever I win the lottery, I donate the money."

Given the habitual nature of the と-clause, it is often used to describe conditions that lead to universal or inevitable consequences when explaining rules and procedures, or giving directions. Here are some examples to illustrate such usage:

<ruby>小<rt>こ</rt></ruby><ruby>切<rt>ぎ</rt></ruby><ruby>手<rt>って</rt></ruby>を<ruby>使<rt>つか</rt></ruby>うと、<ruby>手数料<rt>てすうりょう</rt></ruby>がかかります。
"If you use a check, there is a service charge."

このボタンを<ruby>押<rt>お</rt></ruby>すと、おつりが<ruby>出<rt>で</rt></ruby>てきます。
"If you push the button, change comes out."

あの<ruby>角<rt>かど</rt></ruby>を<ruby>曲<rt>ま</rt></ruby>がると、<ruby>銀行<rt>ぎんこう</rt></ruby>があります。
"If you turn that corner, you will see a bank."

If you rephrase these with either a たら- or ば-clause, the sentences will take on slightly different nuances. With a たら-clause, the sentences acquire the sense of surprise or discovery. With a ば-clause, it is implied that the condition is the minimal necessary effort.

Unlike the たら- or ば-clause, the と-clause cannot be followed by expressions of volition, desire, or instructions at all. This is because the condition-consequence sequence must be predetermined when you use a と-clause.

× <ruby>今月<rt>こんげつ</rt></ruby>の<ruby>給料<rt>きゅうりょう</rt></ruby>をもらうと、スーツを<ruby>買<rt>か</rt></ruby>うつもりです。
(*intended*: "When I get this month's salary, I plan to buy a suit.")

× <ruby>安<rt>やす</rt></ruby>いと、<ruby>買<rt>か</rt></ruby>いたいです。
(*intended*: "If it's inexpensive, I want to buy it.")

× <ruby>買<rt>か</rt></ruby>いたいと、<ruby>買<rt>か</rt></ruby>って<ruby>下<rt>くだ</rt></ruby>さい。
(*intended*: "If you want to buy it, please buy it.")

However, the と-clause shares one characteristic with the たら-clause, which is not shared by the ば-clause: the と-clause with an eventive predicate also expresses a factual condition when the main predicate is in the past tense.

<ruby>100<rt>ひゃく</rt></ruby>ドルを<ruby>円<rt>えん</rt></ruby>に<ruby>両替<rt>りょうがえ</rt></ruby>すると、<ruby>8000<rt>はっせんえん</rt></ruby>円になりました。
"When I exchanged $100 to yen, it came to ¥8,000."

The difference is that the たら-clause is preferred in speech because it creates the sense of anticipatory excitement whereas the と-clause is preferred in writing to reflectively record what has happened.

Stipulating
conditions

Expressing a goal with a conditional

In Unit 13, we studied how to express purposes using the following pattern:

預金するのには、あの銀行がいいですよ。

"In order to deposit money, that bank would be good."

You can achieve a similar effect using a nominalized clause and a conditional.

預金するのだったら、あの銀行がいいですよ。 [たら-clause]
"If you are going to deposit money, that bank would be good."

預金するのなら、あの銀行がいいですよ。 [ば-clause]
"If you are going to deposit money, that bank would be good."

In speech, の is often shortened to ん in a たら-clause.

預金するんだったら、あの銀行がいいですよ。 [たら-clause]
"If you are going to deposit money, that bank would be good."

In the case of a ば-clause, の can be dropped.

預金するなら、あの銀行がいいですよ。 [ば-clause]
"If you are going to deposit money, that bank would be good."

Other nominal forms indicating intensions or plans also achieve similar effects.

預金するつもりだったら、あの銀行がいいですよ。
"If you are intending to deposit money, that bank would be good."

預金する予定なら、あの銀行がいいですよ。
"If you are planning to deposit money, that bank would be good."

With a plain たら- or ば-clause, the sentences become nonsensical.

× 預金したら、あの銀行がいいですよ。 [たら-clause]
(*intended*: "If you have deposited money, that bank would be good.")

× 預金すれば、あの銀行がいいですよ。 [ば-clause]
(*intended*: "As long as you deposit money, that bank would be good.")

Counterfactuals

Some hypothetical conditions are known to the speaker to be untrue, and therefore are called counterfactual conditions.

私 {だったら/なら}、買わない。
"If it were me, I would not buy it."

1 億円{あったら/あれば}、世界旅行に行きます。
"If I had 100 million yen, I will go on a round-the-world trip."

Sentence final conjunctives such as けど "but" and のに "although" give a clear indication that the conditions are counterfactual.

お金があれば、買うんだけど。
"If I had money, I would buy it, but …"

もっとお金があればいいのに。
"It would be nice if I had more money, but …"

When the entire sentence is in the past tense, a たら-clause with a stative predicate (*see* Unit 2) or a ば-clause is interpreted as a counterfactual condition.

1万円あったら、足りた。
"Had there been ¥10,000, it would have been enough."

貯金しておけば、よかった。
"If I had saved money, it would have been good. (= I should have saved money)."

As we studied earlier in this unit, a たら-clause with an eventive predicate (*see* Unit 2) followed by a past event is normally interpreted as a factual condition.

1万円出したら、足りた。
"When I withdrew ¥10,000, it was enough."

To ensure that a たら-clause with an eventive predicate is interpreted as a counterfactual condition, use [V-て] いる form (*see* Unit 8) and turn the predicate into a stative one. The estimation form だろう (*see* Unit 15) is often added to this type of sentence.

1万円出していたら、足りた(だろう)。
"Had I withdrawn ¥10,000, it would have been enough."

Different conditions, the same consequence: [P-て]も

Different conditions often yield the same consequence. You can use a て-form followed by も to describe such a situation.

小切手を使ったら、手数料がかかります。クレジットカードを使っても、手数料がかかります。
"If you use a personal check, there will be a service charge. If you use a credit card, there will also be a service charge."

You can also juxtapose the alternative conditions.

小切手を使っても、クレジットカードを使っても、手数料がかかります。
"Whether you use a personal check or a credit card, there will be a service charge."

Combined with an indeterminate pronoun (*see* Unit 1), this pattern yields the meaning "no matter ..."

どんなに高くても買いたいです。
"No matter how expensive, I want to buy it."

いくらお金^{かね}があっても足^たりません。

"No matter how much money I have, it won't be enough."

Exercise 18.1

Decide if the bold part is a conditional clause or an embedded sentence.

1. I honestly don't remember **if I saw her that night**.

2. I am wondering **if you said something to offend him**.

3. She would have said something **if she had felt uncomfortable**.

4. Who am I meeting? I will tell you **if you promise me not to tell him**.

Exercise 18.2

Fill in the blanks with the appropriate たら-, ば-, or と-clauses.

Non-past form	たら-clause	ば-clause	と-clause
使^{つか}う			
使^{つか}わない			
読^よむ			
読^よむつもりだ			

Exercise 18.3

Describe the surprising turn of events using a たら-clause.

1. You wrote an email to a famous movie star. → An email from the star came back the following day.

2. You turned to the right. → You were in front of your friend's house.

3. You spoke in Japanese. → You were told that your pronunciation was good.

Exercise 18.4

Following the example, describe your feeling of regret using the counterfactual pattern.

Example

You regret not having been to the party. → パーティに行けばよかった。

You regret having been to the party. → パーティに行かなければよかった。

1. You regret not having eaten more. →

2. You regret not having asked anyone (to seek information). →

3. You regret having met her. →

4. You regret having written the letter. →

Exercise 18.5

Following the example, complete each counterfactual sentence with an appropriate conclusion. You can check the meaning of each passage in the Key to exercises.

Example

パーティに行ったから、勉強できなかった。**もし、行かなければもっと勉強できただろう。**

"Because I went to the party, I could not study. If I had not been to the party, I would have been able to study more."

1. ルームメートが起こしてくれたから、5時に起きられた。ルームメートが起こしてくれなければ、＿＿＿＿＿＿＿＿＿
＿＿＿＿＿＿＿＿＿＿＿＿＿＿＿＿＿＿＿＿。

2. 5時に起きたから、6時の電車に乗れた。5時に＿＿＿＿＿＿
＿＿＿＿＿＿＿＿＿＿＿＿＿＿＿＿＿＿＿＿。

3. 6時の電車に乗れたから、テストの時間に間に合った。＿＿＿＿
＿＿＿＿＿＿＿＿＿＿＿＿＿＿＿＿＿＿＿＿。

Exercise 18.6

Select **all** the appropriate conditional forms. You can check the meaning
of each correct sentence in the Key to exercises.

1. この問題は{難しかったら/難しければ/難しいと}後でして下
さい。

2. その辞書は{使ったら/使えば/使うと}ここに返してください。

3. 日本に{行ったら/行けば/行くと/行くのなら}もっと日本語が
上手になりますよ。

4. レストランでお酒を{飲んだら/飲むのなら/飲むつもりだった
ら}レストランまで車を運転して行ってはいけない。

5. レストランでお酒を{飲んだら/飲むのなら/飲むつもりだった
ら}家まで車を運転して帰ってはいけない。

Exercise 18.7

Answer the hypothetical questions. You can check the meaning of each
question and sample answers in the Key to exercises.

1. 留守のはずのとなりの家から変な音が聞こえたら、あなただっ
たらどうしますか。

2. もし運転していた車が大雪のためにハイウェイで動けなくな
ってしまったら、どうすればいいと思いますか。

Exercise 18.8

Translate the sentences into Japanese.

1. Whether I call him in the morning or in the evening, he is not at home.

2. No matter how many times I call him, he does not answer the phone.

UNIT 19

Indicating conformity to or deviation from expectations

Fortunately, many things turn out exactly as you hope. However, some things inevitably fail to meet your expectation despite all your efforts, and on occasion you may even end up doing things you had no intention of doing. The Japanese language is rich in standardized expressions, many of which are adverbs, indicating conformity to or deviation from expectations. In this unit, we will study some of these expressions.

Conformity to expectations: やはり/やっぱり

The adverb やはり "as expected/after all" and its colloquial and more emotional counterpart やっぱり indicate that a given event or state conforms to the speaker's expectation. Although English has no close adverbial counterpart, やはり/やっぱり is a high-frequency adverb in Japanese.

やっぱり！
"I knew it!"

やはり、彼は来なかった。
"As expected, he didn't come."

In the following contexts, やはり/やっぱり signifies that each statement, conforming to his/her subconscious standard, strikes the speaker as natural:

やっぱり、夏は海だよね!
"Naturally, a beach is the place to be in summer, huh?"

A: 日本食で何が一番好きですか。
   "What do you like the best among Japanese food?"

B: やはり/やっぱり、寿司ですね。
   "*Sushi*, of course."

Another notable use of やはり/やっぱり is to signify that the speaker is revisiting a thought that was entertained but rejected earlier.

やはり、来なければよかった。
"After all, I shouldn't have come."

やっぱり、私が行きます。
"On second thoughts, I will go."

In addition, やっぱり is used as a politeness strategy for starting an objection or counter-argument. It signals that the speaker has given careful thought to what s/he is saying.

やっぱり、それは困ります。
"That is troublesome."

やっぱり、こっちの方が良くない?
"Isn't this one better?"

Deviation from expectations: せっかく/わざわざ

The adverb せっかく is another commonly used adverb that lacks an adverbial or idiomatic English counterpart. Meaning that a compelling amount of effort has been expended with an expectation of a desirable outcome, it often appears in a clause introduced by the **CONNECTIVE** particle combination のに "even though" (discussed below) and accentuates the speaker's regret or frustration when an expected outcome is not reached despite the effort.

せっかく海に来たのに、毎日雨が降っている。
"I set aside the special time to come to the beach, but it has been raining every day."

せっかくクッキーを焼いたのに、誰も食べてくれなかった。
"I took the admirable trouble to bake cookies, but nobody ate them."

The effort need not be the speaker's.

せっかく来てくれたのに、家にいなくてごめんね。
"I am sorry I wasn't home when you took the trouble to visit me."

せっかく also appears frequently as part of a reason clause to motivate further efforts to produce at least some desirable result.

何も見れなかったけど、せっかく来たんだし、何か食べて帰ろうよ。
"Even though we could not see anything, because we've come all the way, let's eat something before going home."

せっかく日本語を勉強しているんだから、一度は日本に行ってみたい。
"Since I am studying Japanese, I would like to visit Japan at least once."

Finally, せっかく can modify a noun to indicate that something is rare or valuable.

せっかくのお休みだから、どこか行こうよ。
"Let's go somewhere to make the best of a precious day off."

せっかくのお誘いですが、ちょっと都合がつきません。
"Thank you for your kind invitation, but I won't be able to make it."

The adverb わざわざ is similar to せっかく in that it also highlights the uncommon nature of the effort, but it differs from せっかく in that it marks the effort as unnecessary rather than compelling.

わざわざ(×せっかく)行く必要はないよ。
"No need to take the trouble to go."

19

Indicating
conformity
to or
deviation
from
expec-
tations

わざわざ(×せっかく)届けて下さって、ありがとうございます。
"(You didn't have to do it, but) thank you very much for taking the trouble to deliver it all the way here."

Anticipation of change: もう/まだ

Japanese children playing the game of "hide and seek" will be heard calling out もういいかい "Are you ready yet?" and まだだよ "Not yet." The adverb もう generally means that some change or action has taken place earlier than expected or is imminent.

もう春になりました。もう雪はありません。
"Spring has already come. There is no more snow."

もう行きますよ。もう8時ですから。
"I am leaving now. 'Cause it's already eight o'clock."

The adverb まだ means that an anticipated change or action has not taken place or is not imminent.

まだ冬です。春までまだ3か月もあります。
"It is still winter. There are still three more months before spring."

まだ行きません。まだ30分あります。
"We are not leaving yet. We still have 30 more minutes."

Depending on the polarity of the main predicate, もう can be translated into "already," "yet," or "any longer," and まだ into "still" or "yet." However, do not be confused by the translations. In order to use them appropriately, just pay attention to whether or not the change has happened or is imminent.

Disjunctive connective: [P-plain^(na)] のに

The connective のに, often translated into "although," derives from the combination of the nominalizer の (*see BJ* Unit 11) and the particle に. It means that the main clause event or state contradicts the speaker's expectation.

For instance, in the following example, the speaker's expectation is that when you have a (nowadays special) chance to wear a 浴衣 "summer kimono," you should have a photo taken.

浴衣を着たのに写真を撮らなかった。
"Even though I wore a *yukata*, I didn't have a photo taken."

This meaning of contradiction between personal expectation and the reality crucially distinguishes のに from simple disjunctive particles けれども and が "but" (*see BJ* Unit 6) and prevents it from being used in a request, command, advice, question, or in asking for permission. Use けれども and its variations (i.e. けれど, けど) instead for such speech acts.

かなり混んでいる{×のに/○けど}行ってみて下さい。 [request]
"Even though it is quite crowded, please give it a try and go."

Similarly, のに is incompatible with expressions of intention.

かなり混んでいる{×のに/○けど}行ってみようと思います。
[intention]
"Even though it is crowded, I will give it a try and go."

Excessive behavior or condition: [V/A-stem] すぎる

The verb すぎる, which literally means "pass through," attaches to a verbal or adjectival stem to create a **COMPOUND VERB** and indicates that some action or state is inappropriately excessive.

スピードを出しすぎないで。
"Don't drive too fast!"

かき氷を食べすぎて、お腹が痛くなりました。
"I've eaten too much shaved ice and now have a stomachache."

このシャツはちょっと大きすぎる。
"This shirt is a little too big."

暑すぎて、勉強できないよ。
"It's so hot that I cannot study."

19

Indicating
conformity
to or
deviation
from
expec-
tations

静かすぎて、落ち着かない。
"It's so quiet that it makes me uneasy."

Note that the stems of いい "good" and ない "absent" are よ and なさ respectively in this context, as shown below:

彼女は人がよすぎて、野心がなさすぎる。
"She is too good natured and has too little ambition."

Unexpected outcome: [V-て] しまう

The verb しまう, which literally means "put away (out of sight)," attaches to the て-form of a verb and indicates that something happens unexpectedly, uncontrollably, or irrevocably.

朝までテレビを見てしまいました。 [unexpectedly]
"I ended up watching TV until the morning."

休みはあっという間に終わってしまった。 [uncontrollably]
"The vacation was over before I knew it."

花瓶を割ってしまいました。 [irrevocably]
"I broke the vase."

The contracted form ちゃう is often used in place of てしまう in casual speech.

早く行かないと終わっちゃうよ。
"If you don't hurry, it will be over."

あ、ケーキ、食べたかった?ごめん、全部食べちゃった。
"Oh, you wanted to eat the cake? Sorry, I finished it all."

Exercise 19.1

Consider the meaning of やはり/やっぱり in each of the following sentences. You can check the meaning of each sentence in the Key to exercises.

1. やっぱり犯人はあいつだったんだ。

2. やはり、この計画は白紙にもどして下さい。

3. やっぱり冬は温泉だよね。

4. 焼き肉がいいかな。いや、やっぱり天ぷらが食べたいな。

Exercise 19.2

Choose between もう and まだ. You can check the meaning of each sentence in the Key to exercises.

1. すみません。{もう/まだ}出来ていません。

2. えっ。{もう/まだ}行っちゃったの。

3. {もう/まだ}赤ちゃんです。寝顔はかわいいです。

4. 船が日本を出てから{もう/まだ}1週間たちました。

5. {もう/まだ}食べられる？私は、{もう/まだ}食べられない。

Exercise 19.3

Choose between のに and けど. If both are possible, indicate that. You can check the meaning of each sentence in the Key to exercises.

1. ちょっと高い{のに/けど}少しだけ買ってみたら?

2. わざわざ遠回りして東大寺を見に行った{のに/けど}修理中で中に入れなかった。

3. せっかく作ってくれた{のに/けど}食べられません。

4. おいしい{のに/けど}食べすぎないでください。

5. みんなが困っている{のに/けど}、自分のことしか考えない人がいる。

Exercise 19.4

Add to the following statements the meaning that the conditions are excessive. You can check the meaning of each answer in the Key to exercises.

1. 今日は寒い。

2. 宿題が多い。

19

Indicating
conformity
to or
deviation
from
expec-
tations

3. 相手チームは強かった。

4. あの人はモラルがない。

Exercise 19.5

Express your regret for your action in the following situations using [V-て] しまった.

1. You ate too much ice cream.

2. You spent too much money.

3. You put too much sugar in the coffee.

4. You boiled pasta for too long.

Exercise 19.6

Fill in the blanks and complete the sentences.

1. ＿＿＿＿＿＿＿すぎるよ。これ以上食べられない。

   "It's too spicy! I can't eat any more."

2. ごめん。＿＿＿＿＿＿すぎてしまった。

   "I am sorry. I said too much."

3. 昨日は、ちょっと＿＿＿＿＿＿しまった。

   "I had too much to drink yesterday."

4. 映画は＿＿＿＿＿＿て、途中で＿＿＿＿＿＿。

   "The movie was too long, and I fell asleep (without knowing it) in the middle."

UNIT 20
Expressing influence over others

We often exert influence over others' actions. For instance, some parents will force their children to eat everything on their plates. A friend may let a close friend drive his car. In this unit, we will study constructions used to describe such relationships from the point of view of the one who exerts the influence and from the point of view of the one who is being affected.

Causative construction

Sentence structure

In this section, we will first study how to form a causative sentence. A full causative sentence contains CAUSER (someone who causes someone or something to act or undergo change), CAUSEE (someone or something whose action or change is caused by someone), and the causative verb form in one of the following patterns:

Causative

Causer = Topic/subj.	Causee		Intransitive V (Causative form)
貧しい親は	小さな子どもを	工場で	働かせた。

Poor parents forced their young offspring to work at factories.

205

Causer = Topic/ subj.	Causee		Intransitive V (Causative form)
さいきん おや 最近の親は	こ 子どもたちに	じゆう いろいろ ところ 自由に色々な所に	い 行かせる。
Contemporary parents let their children go to various places freely.			

Causer = Topic/ subj.	Causee		Transitive V (Causative form)
さいきん おや 最近の親は	こ 子どもに	いえ しごと 家の仕事を	てつだ 手伝わせない。
Contemporary parents don't make/let their young offspring help with household chores.			

In all three patterns, the causer is realized as the topic/subject of the sentence.

The selection of the particle to mark the causee depends on whether there is another direct object in the sentence and on the power relationship between the causer and the causee. If the causee's action is intransitive with no direct object involved, the causee himself/herself may be marked by the direct object particle を.

むかし まず おや ちい こども こうじょう はたら
昔は、貧しい親は、小さな子供を工場で働かせた。
"A long time ago, poor parents forced their young offspring to work at factories."

In this case, the parents are more powerful than the causee, a child, who has no self-motivation.

On the other hand, the causee may be treated as the non-subject agent and marked by the non-subject agent particle に (*see* Unit 5) if their self-motivation is recognized, as in the following:

さいきん おや こども じゆう ところ い
最近の親は、子供たちに自由にいろいろな所に行かせる。
"Contemporary parents let their children go to various places freely."

If the verb is a transitive verb, the direct object particle を is automatically assigned only to the direct object of the verb, and the causee, whether willing or unwilling, must be marked by に.

最近の親は、子供に家の仕事を手伝わせない。
"Contemporary parents don't make/let their children help with household chores."

The following is ungrammatical:

× 最近の親は、子供を家の仕事を手伝わせない。
(*intended*: Contemporary parents don't make/let their children help with household chores."

Make sure not to use a sentence like the following, either:

× 猫を食べさせよう。
(*intended*: "Let's feed the cat.")

The verb 食べる is transitive even when the overt direct object is missing. The only possible (but strange) reading of this sentence is "Let's let/make someone eat a cat."

Causative forms

The formation of causative forms is quite regular. To form a causative form from the dictionary form of a one-row verb, drop る and attach させる.

| 食べる | → | 食べさせる | "force/let someone eat" |
| やめる | → | やめさせる | "force/let someone quit something" |

To form a causative form from the dictionary form of a five-row verb, replace the last *u*-row syllable with a corresponding *a*-row syllable and add せる. (*See* Appendix B for more examples.)

| 座る | → | 座らせる | "force/let someone sit" |
| 使う | → | 使わせる | "force/let someone use something" |

The causative counterparts of the two irregular verbs are as follows:

| する | → | させる | "force/let someone do something" |
| 来る | → | 来させる | "force/let someone come over" |

The derived causative forms conjugate as one-row verbs regardless of the original verb type. The following table shows this using 読ませる "force/let someone read" as the example:

Plain conjugation of causative forms

	Affirmative	Negative
Non-past	読ませる "force/let someone read"	読ませない "will not force/let read"
Past	読ませた "forced/let someone read"	読ませなかった "did not force/let read"

You can add various endings to the basic causative base as in the following:

読ませている	"be forcing/letting someone read"
読ませたい	"want to force/let someone read"
読ませよう	"Let's force/let someone read something."
読ませれば	"provided someone forces/lets someone read"

Use of the causative construction

The causative form is of course obligatory in a causative sentence, but the causer and the causee are often omitted as in the following:

待たせて、ごめん!   "Sorry to have kept you waiting!"

泣かせてしまった。   "I ended up making him cry."

The causative construction is commonly used to seek permission to do something.

僕にもちょっとその本を読ませてくれませんか。
"Won't you please let me have a quick look at the book, too?"

もう少し考えさせて下さい。
"Please let me think about it a little longer."

もう少し考えさせて頂けませんか。
"Would you please let me think about it a little longer?"

It should be noted that the distinction between the "を-causative" and the "に-causative" with intransitive verbs does not exactly coincide with the distinction between "force" and "let" in English. In Japanese society, when a subordinate asks his/her boss for permission to do something, it is a common practice for him/her to play down self-motivation or self-initiative. Therefore, the following request also contains the particle を even though its natural English translation contains "let."

部長、私を行かせて下さい。
"(Department) Chief, please let me go."

The following is acceptable, but it can give the impression that the person asking for permission is overly confident of his/her ability to complete the mission:

部長、私に行かせて下さい。
"Chief, please let me go."

The causative construction is also used to apologize for causing the inconvenience of having to do something.

お待たせしました。
"I am sorry for making you wait."   (*lit.* "I made you wait.")

心配させて、ごめんなさい。
"Sorry for making you worry."

Short forms

There are shorter versions of causative forms, which employ the ending す instead of せる. (*See* Appendix B for more examples.)

食べさせる	→ 食べさす	"force/let someone eat"
飲ませる	→ 飲ます	"force/let someone drink"
させる	→ さす	"force/let someone do"
来させる	→ 来さす	"force/let someone come"

These forms conjugate like five-row verbs.

Plain conjugation of short causative forms

	Affirmative	Negative
Non-past	読_よます "force/let someone read"	読_よまさない "will not force/let read"
Past	読_よました "forced/let someone read"	読_よまさなかった "did not force/let read"

The shorter causative forms tend to be used when the causer acts more directly than merely instructs/permits the causee to act. For example, in the following example, the causer (addressee) would have to hold the milk bottle to the baby's mouth to feed him:

悪_{わる}いけど、この子_こにミルク飲_のまして。

"Sorry to trouble you, but please feed milk to the baby."

Causative-passive

The causative construction can combine with the passive construction that we studied in Unit 5. The causative-passive construction allows the perspective of the one who is forced to do something (i.e. causee) to come to the fore.

Causative passive

Causee = Topic/ subj.	Causer		Transitive V (Causative-passive form)
子_こどもたちは	お父_{とう}さんに	庭仕事_{にわしごと}を	手伝_{てつだ}わせられた。
The children were made to help with the yard work by their father.			

The above sentence is based on the following causative sentence:

Causative

Causer = Topic/subj.	Causee		Transitive V (Causative form)
お父さんは	子どもたちに	庭仕事を	手伝わせた。
The father made the children help with the yard work.			

To formulate the causative-passive sentence, turn the original non-subject causee agent (the children in this case) into the subject by adding が or は, add the passive ending られる to the causative base, and mark the causer (the father) with the particle に.

Because the causative forms are one-row verbs, the formation of causative-passive forms is very regular. Just add られる to the causative base.

食べさせる → 食べさせられる   "be forced to eat"

飲ませる → 飲ませられる   "be forced to drink"

Causative-passive forms thus created are again one-row verbs.

In standard Japanese, the short causative forms of one-row and irregular verbs are generally avoided in causative-passive forms, probably to avoid the さ さ sequence.

食べさす → × 食べさされる

On the other hand, the short causative forms of five-row verbs are often preferred to their long counterparts in causative-passive forms, especially in colloquial speech.

飲ます → ○ 飲まされる "be forced to drink"

In addition to describing an event from a different participant's perspective, the causative-passive construction is frequently used to indicate that a strong external stimulus triggers a thought or emotion. The simple causative counterparts are avoided for this purpose.

あの映画には、感動させられました。
"I was moved by that movie." (= That movie moved me.)

今<ruby>でも<rt></rt></ruby>子供が工場で働いているという話には、考えさせられます。

"I am made to think by the story that even now children work in factories."

(= The story that even now children work in factories makes me pensive.)

The [V-て] もらう construction, which we studied in *BJ* Unit 24, has a structure and meaning similar to that of the に causative.

お父さんは、子供たちに庭仕事を手伝ってもらった。

"The father had his children help with the yard work (and was grateful)."

However, the [V-て] もらう construction does not have a passive counterpart. Do not try to turn the above sentence into a passive sentence.

Adversity passive

In Unit 5, we studied passive sentences such as the following:

この本は、世界の子供たちに読まれている。

"This book is being read by children all over the world."

Japanese has another type of passive that utilizes the same passive verb forms explained in Unit 5. This new passive, exemplified below, has no direct counterpart in English. Meaning that the subject of the sentence is adversely or emotionally affected by someone else's action, this construction is commonly known as the **ADVERSITY PASSIVE**.

Adversity passive

Affected = Topic/subj.	Agent		V (Passive form)
子どもは	母親に	お小遣いを	とりあげられた。
The child was upset by his mother taking his allowance away.			

In the above example, the agent, the one who takes away the money, is marked by the particle に. However, お小遣い "allowance," the direct object of the verb とる "take," does not turn into the subject. Instead, another party, the child, is added as the subject.

Since the formation of this type of passive does not involve turning a direct object into a subject, the verb can also be intransitive (*see* Unit 2) as shown below.

母親は、子供に泣かれた。
"The mother was emotionally affected by the child crying."

子供は、金魚に死なれて泣いた。
"The child's goldfish died, and he cried."

The actor can also be a self-propelling force such as rain.

橋本さんは、会社帰りに雨に降られた。
"It rained on Mr. Hashimoto on his way home from work (to his inconvenience)."

The adversity passive construction is often accompanied by [V-て] しまう, the out-of-control pattern we studied in Unit 19. The combination highlights the unfortunate nature of the event.

橋本さんは、会社帰りに雨に降られてしまった。
"It ended up raining on Mr. Hashimoto on his way home from work (to his inconvenience)."

Note that causative sentences and adversity passive sentences look very similar. If you use the particle に for the non-subject agent, the only apparent difference between the two is the consonants. The *s* sound appears in the causative sentence and the *r* sound in the adversity passive sentence.

私は猫に魚を食べさせた。 [causative]
"I let the cat eat a fish."

弟は妹に手紙を読ませた。 [causative]
"My younger brother made/let my younger sister read the letter."

213

私 は猫に 魚 を食べられた。 [adversity passive]

"I was upset by the cat eating the fish."

弟 は 妹 に手紙を読まれた。 [adversity passive]

"My younger brother was upset by my younger sister reading the letter."

Exercise 20.1

Change the following verbs into long causative forms.

1. やめる "stop/quit"　　　＿＿＿＿＿＿＿＿

2. 払う "pay"　　　　　　＿＿＿＿＿＿＿＿

3. 勉強する "study"　　　＿＿＿＿＿＿＿＿

4. 持って来る "bring"　　＿＿＿＿＿＿＿＿

Exercise 20.2

Fill in the blanks with に or を and translate the sentence into English.

1. 僕(　　)行かせて! (a boy asserting that he is more fit for the task than his sister)

2. 今からホテルの者(　　)そちらにうかがわせます。

3. シェフ(　　)今すぐこの 魚 (　　)料理させましょう。

4. 先に子供(　　)食べさせました。

Exercise 20.3

Following the example, fill in the blanks with appropriate forms of the verbs given in the brackets. You can check the meaning of each sentence in the Key to exercises.

Example

[入る] → 中に**入らせて**下さい。 "Please let me go inside."

1. [払う]　　　　→ 私 に＿＿＿＿＿＿下さい。

2. [休む]　　　　→ ちょっとここで＿＿＿＿＿下さい。

3. [撮る]　　　→　写真を＿＿＿＿＿下さい。

4. [ご紹介する]　→　＿＿＿＿＿＿＿＿下さい。

5. [読む]　　　→　＿＿＿＿＿＿＿＿頂けますか。

6. [置く]　　　→　ここに荷物を＿＿＿＿＿頂けますか。

Exercise 20.4

Translate the sentences into English.

1. 受付の列が長くていらいらさせられました。
2. 今度の旅行では、いろいろ勉強させられました。

Exercise 20.5

Choose **all** the appropriate forms from the options in the brackets and translate the sentences.

1. コンピューターがこわれたので、{直させた/直された/直してもらった}。
2. 旅行中、パスポートを{ぬすませて/ぬすまれて/ぬすんでもらって}大変だった。
3. 今朝5時に母に{起こさせた/起こされた/起こしてもらった}ので、飛行機に間に合った。
4. 重い荷物を{持たせて/持たれて/持ってもらって}ごめん。

Exercise 20.6

The following sentences are intended to describe some unfortunate circumstances that Mr. Smith experienced during his family vacation. Change each verb in the parentheses into an appropriate form and explain what the unfortunate circumstance was.

1. スミスさんは飛行機の中で子供に(泣く)しまいました。
2. スミスさんは、ホテルで子供に中から鍵を(かける)しまいました。

3. スミスさんは、レンタカーのトランクに入れておいたカメラを
(ぬすむ)しまいました。

4. スミスさんは、レストランで高い料金を(とる)しまいま
した。

Exercise 20.7

Translate the following passage into English.

テレビの番組に関して「やらせ」ということが問題になる
ことがある。これは、ドキュメンタリー番組などを作る人
が、話をおもしろくするために、番組に出て来る人に何か
をやらせたり言ってもらったりすることだ。「泣かせる
話」を簡単に作り出したり、視聴者を笑わせるために、す
るのだ。これは許されることなのだろうか。考えさせられ
る。

APPENDIX A

Accent

Accent in Japanese distinguishes words and characterizes word classes as well as certain grammatical constructions. This appendix summarizes some notable points concerning Japanese accent.

Stress versus pitch accent

English accent is "stress-based." That is, English accent is marked by the change in loudness, length, and pitch level.

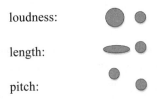

loudness:

length:

pitch:

The following diagram illustrates the combined effect of loudness, length, and pitch on a two-syllable word with a stressed initial syllable:

stress:

This stress system induces English speakers to use stress accent even for a word of Japanese origin such as *sushi* and *sashimi*.

sushi   *sashimi*

However, Japanese accent is realized primarily by manipulating the pitch level. As Japanese words, *sushi* and *sashimi*, for instance, should be pronounced in the following manner:

すし   さしみ

Try to control your pitch level without changing the loudness or length of syllables.

Marking an accent

In standard Japanese, accent is realized as a significant fall in the pitch level. In the word 朝 "morning," the first syllable is pronounced high, and the second significantly lower. The word is considered to have an accent on the first syllable.

あさ   "morning"

The word 料理 "cooking" also has an accent on the first syllable, but in this case the pitch falls between the first and the second mora of the long syllable りょう.

りょうり   "cooking"

Words can be distinguished solely on the basis of the presence or absence of an accent. For instance, 未知 accented on the initial syllable means "unknown yet," whereas 道 without an accent means "road."

みち   "unknown yet"

みち   "road"

The pitch rise between the first and the second mora of unaccented 道 "road" is automatic and predictable because the pitch always rises after a short and unaccented initial syllable. If the initial syllable is long and unaccented, as in 教会 "church," the pitch rises after the first mora when very carefully pronounced. However, in normal speech, the pitch for such words starts out high and remains level.

きょうかい   or   きょうかい "church"

This automatic pitch rise is also observed with words that are accented on a syllable other than the first.

‾‾	
たまご	"egg"
‾‾‾	
スカート	"skirt"
‾‾‾‾	
かたつむり	"snail"

The three pitch patterns that we have seen so far—falling, rising (or level), and rising (or level) followed by a fall—exhaust all the possible pitch patterns for standard Japanese words. Importantly, a Japanese word cannot have more than one accented syllable, and within a single word the pitch will not rise again after an accented syllable. Therefore, in order to tell which of the three contours a word exhibits, we only need to indicate the location of an accent, which we will mark with a backslash hereafter, as in the following:

たま\ご   "egg"

Accent types of nouns

Nouns consisting of one syllable are either accented or unaccented. For instance, 脳 のう "brain" is accented, whereas 能 のう "Noh theater" is unaccented.

脳 の\う   "brain"

能 のう   "Noh theater"

Even nouns consisting of one short syllable, such as 木 "tree" and 気 "mind," are either accented or unaccented, although they cannot be distinguished when pronounced on their own.

木 き\   "tree"

気 き   "mind"

The contrast between these two words shows up when a particle, for instance が, is attached.

木が大きい	き\がおおき\い	"The tree is big."
気が大きい	きがおおき\い	"S/he is magnanimous."

219

Similarly, nouns consisting of two syllables are either accented on the first syllable or on the second syllable, or unaccented. The contrast between one that is accented on the short second syllable and one that is unaccented becomes clear when a particle is attached.

箸	は\し	"chopsticks"
橋	はし\	"bridge"
端	はし	"edge"
橋に座った	はし\に すわった	"I sat on the bridge."
端に座った	はしにすわった	"I sat on the edge/border."

In principle, this pattern holds true with nouns of any length. You must remember if a noun is accented or unaccented, and, if accented, on which syllable, because all syllables are potential accent bearers. However, a large number of nouns three or more syllables long are either unaccented or accented on the syllable containing the third mora from the end. This is particularly true of loan words. For instance, the US state names are largely divided into the following two groups:

(i) unaccented:

アラバマ	"Alabama"
カリフォルニア	"California"
コロラド	"Colorado"
フロリダ	"Florida"

(ii) accented on the syllable containing the third mora from the end:

アーカ\ンソー	"Arkansas"
コネチカ\ット	"Connecticut"
ケンタ\ッキー	"Kentucky"
ワシ\ントン	"Washington"

Accent types of verbs

Verbs are also divided into accented and unaccented groups. Generally speaking, the dictionary forms of all accented verbs have an accent on the syllable containing the second mora from the end.

食べる	たべ\る	"eat"
通る	と\おる	"pass"
切る	き\る	"cut"

The dictionary forms of unaccented verbs have no accent.

変える	かえる	"change"
聞く	きく	"listen"
着る	きる	"wear"

Accent types of い-adjectives

In principle, い-adjectives are also divided into accented and unaccented ones.

| 安い | やす\い |
| 冷たい | つめたい |

However, the distinction between accented and unaccented い-adjectives is gradually being lost in favor of the accented pattern.

Accent types of な-adjectives

な-adjectives are like nouns. For instance, two-syllable な-adjectives can be accented on the initial or second syllable, or unaccented.

不利な	ふ\りな	"disadvantageous"
地味な	じみ\な	"subdued"
健康な	けんこうな	"healthy"

Accent and focus

Above, we saw that Japanese accent characterizes word classes and that there are accented and unaccented types in each class. Japanese accent also has the function of separating focal elements. The lack of accent can mean less focus or familiarity. For instance, a dramatic onomatopoeic adverb such as ガラガラと "rumbling" has an accent on the initial syllable, whereas its derived adjectival counterpart ガラガラの "vacuous" is unaccented.

| ガ\ラガラと | "rumbling" |
| ガラガラの | "vacuous" |

Familiar words or words signifying psychological closeness tend to become unaccented. Accented 彼氏 means "he" or "boyfriend." Unaccented 彼氏 can only mean "boyfriend."

| 彼氏 | か\れし | "he, boyfriend" |
| | かれし | "boyfriend" |

A grammatical unit that is dependent on others may also become unaccented. In Unit 1 of this book, we see that indeterminate pronouns are pronounced either with an initial accent or without an accent depending on the meaning. The unaccented option along with a negative marker forms an accentual phrase. The total phrase is pronounced with an initial rise and an accent on the negative form.

　　どこにもな\い。　　　　"It is nowhere to be seen."

On the other hand, the accented indeterminate pronoun can appear either with a positive or a negative form because it does not form a grammatical construction with either.

　　ど\こにもあ\る。　　　"It is everywhere."

　　ど\こにもな\い。　　　"It is non-existent everywhere.'

APPENDIX B

Basic conjugations

Basic conjugations of five-row verbs

* Irregular conjugations   ( ) Forms that are not usually used.

	Plain, negative, non-past	Plain, negative, past	Passive	Causative	Short causative	Polite, non-past
say	言わない	言わなかった	言われる	言わせる	言わす	言います
wait	待たない	待たなかった	待たれる	待たせる	待たす	待ちます
return	帰らない	帰らなかった	帰られる	帰らせる	帰らす	帰ります
read	読まない	読まなかった	読まれる	読ませる	読ます	読みます
call	呼ばない	呼ばなかった	呼ばれる	呼ばせる	呼ばす	呼びます
die	死なない	死ななかった	死なれる	死なせる	死なす	死にます
speak	話さない	話さなかった	話される	話させる	話さす	話します
write	書かない	書かなかった	書かれる	書かせる	書かす	書きます
swim	泳がない	泳がなかった	泳がれる	泳がせる	泳がす	泳ぎます
go	行かない	行かなかった	行かれる	行かせる	行かす	行きます
exist	ない*	なかった*				あります
be/come/go (honorific)	いらっしゃらない	いらっしゃらなかった	(いらっしゃられる)	(いらっしゃらせる)	(いらっしゃらす)	いらっしゃいます

Plain, non-past	ば-conditional	Potential	Imperative	Volitional	Plain, past	て-form
言う	言えば	言える	言え	言おう	言った	言って
待つ	待てば	待てる	待て	待とう	待った	待って
帰る	帰れば	帰れる	帰れ	帰ろう	帰った	帰って
読む	読めば	読める	読め	読もう	読んだ	読んで
呼ぶ	呼べば	呼べる	呼べ	呼ぼう	呼んだ	呼んで

死ぬ	死ねば	死ねる	死ね	死のう	死んだ	死んで
話す	話せば	話せる	話せ	話そう	話した	話して
書く	書けば	書ける	書け	書こう	書いた	書いて
泳ぐ	泳げば	泳げる	泳げ	泳ごう	泳いだ	泳いで
行く	行けば	行ける	行け	行こう	行った*	行って*
ある	あれば		(あれ)	(あろう)	あった	あって
いらっしゃる	いらっしゃれば	いらっしゃれる	いらっしゃい*	(いらっしゃろう)	いらっしゃった	いらっしゃって

Basic conjugations of one-row verbs

	Plain, negative, non-past	Plain, negative, past	Passive	Causative	Short causative	Polite, non-past
eat	食べない	食べなかった	食べられる	食べさせる	食べさす	食べます

Plain, non-past	ば-conditional	Potential	Imperative	Volitional	Plain, past	て-form
食べる	食べれば	食べられる	食べろ	食べよう	食べた	食べて

Basic conjugations of irregular verbs

	Plain, negative, non-past	Plain, negative, past	Passive	Causative	Short causative	Polite, non-past
come	来ない	来なかった	来られる	来させる	来さす	来ます
do	しない	しなかった	される	させる	さす	します

Plain, non-past	ば-conditional	Potential	Imperative	Volitional	Plain, past	て-form
来る	来れば	来られる	来い	来よう	来た	来て
する	すれば	できる	しろ	しよう	した	して

Basic conjugations of polite forms

	Non-past	Non-past, negative	Past	Past, negative	Volitional
say	言います	言いません	言いました	言いませんでした	言いましょう
eat	食べます	食べません	食べました	食べませんでした	食べましょう

Basic conjugations of い-adjectives

	Plain, non-past	Plain, negative, non-past	Plain, past	Plain, negative, past	ば-conditional	Adverbial
big	大きい	大きくない	大きかった	大きくなかった	大きければ	大きく
good	いい	よくない	よかった	よくなかった	よければ	よく

て-form	Pre-nominal	Polite, non-past	Polite, negative, non-past	Polite, past	Polite, negative, past
大きくて	大きい	大きいです	大きくないです 大きくありません	大きかったです	大きくなかったです 大きくありませんでした
よくて	いい	いいです	よくないです よくありません	よかったです	よくなかったです よくありませんでした

Basic conjugations of な-adjectives

	Plain, non-past	Plain, negative, non-past	Plain, past	Plain, negative, past	ば-conditional	Adverbial
quiet	静かだ	静かではない 静かじゃない	静かだった	静かではなかった 静かじゃなかった	静かなら(ば) 静かであれば	静かに

て-form	Pre-nominal	Polite, non-past	Polite, negative, non-past	Polite, past	Polite, negative, past
静かで	静かな	静かです	静かではないです 静かじゃないです 静かではありません 静かじゃありません	静かでした	静かではなかったです 静かじゃなかったです 静かではありませんでした 静かじゃありませんでした

Basic conjugations of noun + copula

	Plain, non-past	Plain, negative, non-past	Plain, past	Plain, negative, past	ば-conditional	Adverbial
(be) a student	学生<ruby>学生<rt>がくせい</rt></ruby>だ	学生じゃない 学生ではない	学生だった	学生ではなかった 学生じゃなかった	学生なら(ば) 学生であれば	学生に

て-form	Pre-nominal	Polite, non-past	Polite, negative, non-past	Polite, past	Polite, negative, past
学生で	学生の 学生である	学生です	学生ではないです 学生じゃないです 学生ではありません 学生じゃありません	学生でした	学生ではなかったです 学生じゃなかったです 学生ではありませんでした 学生じゃありませんでした

APPENDIX C

Summary of grammatical contexts for plain forms, て-forms, and stem forms

This appendix summarizes where to use (i) plain forms, (ii) て-forms, and (iii) stem forms.

The following notations are used to refer to predicate types:

P   All types of predicates (i.e. verbs, い/な-adjectives, noun + copula)
V   Verbs
A   い/な-adjectives

The contexts where plain forms are used also allow polite forms under certain conditions. Specific contexts are noted as follows:

- Context that allows polite forms in polite speech
° Context that allows polite forms in extra-polite speech
Context that requires polite forms in polite speech

The non-past affirmative form of the copula when it must be changed to something other than だ is specified in the parentheses.

BJ refers to the companion volume *Basic Japanese: A Grammar and Workbook*. *IJ* refers to this book.

Grammatical contexts that require plain forms

Either non-past or past plain forms

Reason, background, information, contrast

P•	から	北風が吹いているから、寒いです。 "Because the north wind is blowing, it is cold."	BJ5
P•	けど	窓から 光 が入るけど、あまり明るくない。 "Although light comes in from the window, it is not very bright."	BJ5
P#	が	窓から 光 が入るが、あまり明るくない。 "Although light comes in from the window, it is not very bright."	BJ5
P°	～し、 ～し、	天気がいいし、 暖 かいし、散歩に行こう。 "It's sunny and warm, so let's go for a walk."	IJ9
P°*(na)*	のに₁	もう四月なのに、雪が降っている。 "Even though it's already April, it's snowing."	IJ19
P•*(na)*	ので	風邪なので、今日は休みます。 "I have a cold, so I will take a day off."	BJ23
Non-vol. P *(no/na)*	ために₁	台風が来たために、キャンセルになった。 "Because a typhoon came, it was cancelled."	IJ13
P	からだ	寒いです。北風が吹いているからです。 "It is cold. That's because the north wind is blowing."	BJ23

Indirect quotation

P	と	ニュースで山^{やま}では紅葉^{こうよう}がはじまったと言^いっていました。 "They were reporting on the news that leaves were beginning to change color in the mountains."	*IJ16*
P	そうだ	山^{やま}では紅葉^{こうよう}がはじまったそうです。 "I heard that leaves have begun to change color in the mountains."	*IJ16*
P	か	山^{やま}はもう寒^{さむ}いか聞^きいてください。 "Please ask if it is already cold in the mountains."	*IJ16*

Noun and nominalizer

P°(no/na)	Noun	あそこに見^みえる滝^{たき} "The waterfall that you can see over there"	*BJ4*
P°(da to iu/na)	こと	昔^{むかし}ここに湖^{みずうみ}があったことはあまり知^しられていません。 "It is not widely known that there used to be a lake here a long time ago."	*BJ11*
P°(na)	の	冬^{ふゆ}にその滝^{たき}まで行^いくのは危険^{きけん}です。 "It is dangerous to go to that waterfall in winter."	*BJ11*

Estimation

P(no/na)	ようだ	川^{かわ}に鮭^{さけ}がもどって来^きたようだ。 "It appears that salmon have come back to the river."	*IJ15*
P(no/na)	はずだ	環境^{かんきょう}はあまり悪^{わる}くないはずだ。 "My understanding is that the ecological environment is not too bad."	*IJ15*
P(da-drop)	だろう	この水^{みず}は飲^のめるだろう。 "You can probably drink this water."	*IJ15*

P^(da -drop)	かも しれない	これは新種のキノコ<u>かもしれない</u>。 "This may be a new kind of mushroom."	IJ15
P^(da -drop)	らしい	川の水がきれいになった<u>らしい</u>。 "It looks like the river water has become clean."	IJ15
P^(da -drop)	みたいだ	あの雲はアイスクリーム<u>みたいだ</u>ね。 "That cloud looks like (a scoop of) ice cream."	IJ15
P^(da -drop)	かしら／ かな	明日は晴れる<u>かしら</u>。 "I wonder if it will clear up tomorrow."	IJ6

Other

V°	より／ ほう	池で遊ぶ<u>より</u>川で遊ぶ<u>方</u>がおもしろい。 "It is more fun to play in the river than in the pond."	BJ18
P°^(da -drop)	なら	山へ行く<u>なら</u>、雨具を持って行った<u>方</u>がいいよ。 "If you are going to the mountain, you should take rain gear."	IJ18

Only non-past forms

Conditions and timing I

P°	と	火山が爆発する<u>と</u>、ここにも灰が降ってくる。 "When the volcano erupts, ash falls here, too."	IJ18
V°	まえに	出発する<u>前に</u>、ガソリンを入れておいて下さい。 "Please fill up the tank before we leave."	BJ12 IJ4
V°	うちに	大きな波が来ない<u>うちに</u>浜からあがった。 "Before large waves arrived, we left the beach."	IJ4

V	あいだ	君がサーフィンをしている間、僕は浜で寝るよ。 "I will take a nap on the beach while you are surfing."	IJ4
V	ところだ₁	これから、ハイキングに行くところです。 "We are about to go hiking now."	IJ4

Plain, decision, and change

V	つもりだ	来月、車を買うつもりです。 "I plan to buy a car next month."	IJ12
V	ようにする	毎日、野菜を食べるようにしている。 "I am making sure to eat vegetables every day."	IJ14
V	ようになる	漢字がたくさん読めるようになった。 "I can read many *kanji* now."	IJ14
V	ことにする	たばこを止めることにした。 "I decided to quit smoking."	IJ14
V	ことになる	東京に転勤することになった。 "It's been decided that I transfer to the Tokyo office."	IJ14

Purpose

V	のに₂	新幹線に乗るのに、1万円かかる。 "It costs ¥10,000 to ride the bullet train."	IJ19
Vol. V	ために₂	家を買うために、貯金している。 "I am saving to buy a house."	IJ13
Non-vol. V/A⁽ⁿᵃ⁾	ように	けがをしないように、気をつけて。 "Be careful so you won't get hurt."	IJ13

Other

V	ことが できる	兄はセスナを操縦することができる。 "My elder brother can fly small airplanes."	*BJ16*
P^(no/na)	ことが ある₁	平日に映画を見ることがある。 "I sometimes watch a movie on a week day."	*IJ17*

Only past forms

Condition and timing II

V°	ら	雨が降ったら、行きません。 "If it rains, I won't go."	*IJ18*
V	あとで	滝を見た後、昼ごはんを食べた。 "After we saw the waterfall, we ate lunch."	*BJ12* *IJ4*
V	ところだ₂	さっき出かけたところです。 "S/he has just left home."	*IJ4*
V	ばかり	食べたばかりで、お腹がすいていない。 "I just ate, so I'm not hungry."	*IJ4*

Other

P	〜り、〜り する	海で泳いだり、日光浴をしたりした。 "I did such things as swimming in the ocean and sunbathing."	*IJ9*
P^(no/na)	ことがある₂	この湖は凍ったことがない。 "This lake has never been frozen over."	*IJ17*

Grammatical contexts that require て-forms

Close linkage

P	(、)	川は幅が広くて長い。[similar attributes] "The river is wide and long."	*BJ6*
P	(、)	空は青くて、雲は白い。 [contrasting situations] "The sky is blue, and the clouds are white."	*BJ6*
P	(、)	霧が深くて前がよく見えない。[cause] "The fog is dense, and I cannot see the area before me well."	*BJ23*
V°	(、)	丘を越えて、キャンプ場に着いた。 [sequence of events] "We crossed the hill and arrived at the campground."	*BJ6*
V°	(、)	布団をかぶって、寝た。[manner and action] "I slept with a quilt pulled over my head."	*BJ6*
V°	(、)	コンパスを使って滝をさがした。[means] "Using a compass, I looked for the waterfall."	*BJ6*
V	から	テントを張ってから焚き火をたいた。 "After pitching the tent, we started a fire."	*BJ12*

Basis of apology, appreciation, and judgment

P°	(、)	枝を折ってしまってすみません。[apology] "I am sorry for breaking the branch."	*BJ25*
P	(も)いい	疲れた！テントで休んでいい? "I am exhausted. Can I rest in the tent?" その宿題は月曜日まで出さなくてもいいです。 "You don't have to turn in that homework until Monday."	*BJ21*

P	はいけない	まだ食べてはいけない。	BJ21
		"You may not eat yet."	
		早く食べなくてはいけない。	
		"You must eat quickly."	
V°	(、)	花を届けてくださってありがとうございました。[appreciation]	BJ25
		"Thank you for bringing the flowers."	

Before an auxiliary verb or adjective

V	いる	花の種をまいています。	BJ6
		"I am sowing flower seeds."	IJ2,8
		花がさいています。	
		"The flowers are in bloom."	
V	ある	じゃまになるから長い枝は切ってあります。	IJ8
		"Because they would be in the way, I have cut off long branches."	
V	おく	木を植えるために大きな穴を掘っておきました。	IJ13
		"In order to plant a tree, I dug a big hole in preparation."	
V	ください	そこは踏まないで下さい。	BJ20
		"Please don't step on there."	
V	あげる	母のために庭を掃除してあげました。	BJ24
		"I swept the yard for my mother."	
V	くれる	水をまいてくれませんか。	BJ24
		"Will you sprinkle water for me?"	
V	もらう	花を植えてもらいました。	BJ24
		"Will you sprinkle water for me?"	
V	みる	中まで焼けたか見てみて下さい。	IJ17
		"Please check and see if it's cooked through."	

234

V	しまう	お腹がいっぱいになって<u>しまった</u>。	IJ19
		"I've become so full (that I can't eat anything else)."	
V	ほしい	子供たちには庭の草をとって<u>ほしい</u>。	IJ11
		"I want the children to weed the garden."	
V	いく	駅前のコンビニでお弁当を買って<u>行く</u>。	IJ13
		"I will buy my lunch at the convenience store in front of the station on my way."	
V	くる	日本でよく日本語を勉強して<u>来</u>ます。	IJ13
		"I will come back having studied Japanese well in Japan."	

Grammatical contexts that require stem forms

Before polite endings and in honorifics

V	ます	明日は山登りに<u>行き</u><u>ます</u>。	BJ6
		"I am going to hike up a mountain tomorrow."	
V	ましょう	今年の冬は、この山に<u>登り</u><u>ましょう</u>。	BJ19
		"Let's climb this mountain this winter."	
V	ませんか	そして、来年は、あの山に挑戦<u>し</u><u>ません</u><u>か</u>。	BJ19
		"And why don't we try that mountain next year?"	
V	お〜になる	先生は、80才で、富士山の頂上まで<u>お歩き</u><u>になった</u>そうです。	BJ10
		"I heard that the professor walked to the top of Mt. Fuji at the age of 80."	
V	お〜する	帰りは私が先生を<u>お送り</u><u>します</u>。	BJ10
		"I will give the professor a ride on the way back."	

Before an auxiliary verb or adjective

V	はじめる	山に登り始めたのは１０才の時です。 "It was when I was 10 that I began mountain climbing."	IJ14
V	なさい	ちょっと、待ちなさい。 "Wait!"	IJ10
V/A	すぎる	今日は、歩きすぎた。もう足が痛すぎて、これ以上歩けない。 "I walked too far today. My legs hurt too much, and I can no longer walk."	IJ19
A	がる	私の犬は地震を怖がるし、どこにでも穴を掘りたがります。 "My dog is scared of earthquakes. Moreover, he wants to dig holes everywhere."	BJ15
V	にくい	凍った道はこの靴では歩きにくい。 "A frozen road is difficult to walk on wearing these shoes."	BJ22
V	やすい	霧が晴れて、前が見やすくなった。 "The fog cleared, and the visibility improved."	BJ22
V	たい	富士山に登りたい。 "I want to climb Mt. Fuji."	BJ18
V/A	そうだ	日が暮れそうです。寒そうな夕日です。 "The sun will be gone any moment. It is a cold-looking sunset."	IJ15

Other

V	かた	頂上への行き方を調べておいた。 "I checked how to get to the top of the mountain in advance."	*IJ3*
V	ながら	時々、後ろを振り返りながら、歩いた。 "I walked while looking back from time to time."	*IJ4*
V	に(行く)	頂上からの朝日を見に行ったんです。 "I went to see the view of the sun rise from the top of the mountain."	*IJ13*
A	さ	カーナビの便利さに慣れると、道を覚えなくなる。 "When you get used to the convenience of GPS, you stop bothering to learn the roads."	*BJ3*

KEY TO EXERCISES

Unit 1

Exercise 1.1
1　何も買いませんでした
2　誰にも聞きませんでした
3　どこにも行きませんでした

Exercise 1.2
1　誰 "Did any students come in the morning?" "Yes, a graduate student came."
2　何 "Have you seen any entertaining movies recently?" "Yes, I have seen a movie called 'The Magic.'"
3　どこ "Do you know of any inexpensive shoe stores?" "Let me see. The supermarket in front of the station also carries inexpensive shoes."

Exercise 1.3
1　か, も "Did someone answer the phone?" "No, nobody did."
2　かから, からも "Was there a call from someone?" "No, there wasn't any call from anyone."
3　かに(かへ is also acceptable), にも (へも is also acceptable) "Did you go anywhere on Sunday?" "No, I didn't go anywhere."

Exercise 1.4
1　も飲みたくありません "There is coffee as well as black tea, but I don't want to drink either."
2　も見たくありません "There is a TV in the room, but I don't want to watch any (program)."
3　にも行きたくありません (へも行きたくありません is also acceptable) "The weather is nice outside, but I don't want to go anywhere."
4　にも会いたくありません "A friend is coming over, but to tell you the truth, I don't want to see anyone."

Exercise 1.5

1 も "I need two, so I will buy both."

2 か "I don't have much money, so I can only buy one of the two."

3 も "Because they were very expensive, I didn't buy either of them."

4 でも "Whichever of the two will do, so please buy one of them."

Exercise 1.6

1 行きます "Ms. Kato loves old rugs. In search of old ones, she goes anywhere."

2 買います "Mr. Kimura's hobby is collecting various maps. When a secondhand bookstore carries some, he buys all of them at once (no matter how many)."

3 書いて "Because *kanji* are difficult, I memorize them by writing them any number of times."

4 電話します "Professor Tanaka's research group is conducting market research now. Because they need a large amount of data, looking for people who will answer the questions, each member calls no matter how many tens of people every day."

Unit 2

Exercise 2.1

1 CLV "A taxi stopped in front of the house."

2 AV "Let's walk over to the station."

3 CSV "The door closed."

4 AV "You can open this wine bottle with (a flick of) the wrist."

5 CSV "The power source of the personal computer was disconnected."

6 CSV "I got married last month."

7 CLV "Where shall we go tomorrow?"

8 AV "Those of you who have questions, please raise your hands."

9 CLV "I am happy because my grades have gone up this semester."

10 AV "I went to Alaska and saw an aurora."

Exercise 2.2

1 non-volitional subject 2 volitional subject 3 non-volitional subject
4 volitional subject 5 non-volitional subject 6 volitional subject
7 volitional subject 8 volitional subject 9 non-volitional subject
10 volitional subject

Exercise 2.3

1 閉める 2 開ける 3 消す 4 止める 5 直す 6 返す 7 変える
8 起こす 9 始める 10 落とす

Exercise 2.4

1 消して "Turn off the TV before going to bed, will you?"
2 始まる "When is the summer vacation starting?"
3 つけ "It's cold. So, let's turn on the heater."
4 治って "I am glad that your cold is gone."
5 直して "Please revise this composition once more."
6 切って "We cut the cake into quarters and ate it."
7 起こして "If I don't wake up by seven, wake me up, will you?"
8 出す "In Japan, they put out trash after sorting it into combustible and non-combustible trash."

Exercise 2.5

1 開かない, 開け "The lid of this bottle is so tight that I cannot open it. Yoko, can you open it?"
2 見る, 見え "Though we came to view the fireworks, there were too many tall buildings (in the way), and we couldn't see them at all, could we?"
3 出, 出して "Sweetie, Jiro wants to go outside, so let him out, please?"
4 止まら, 止めて "(Help), I can't stop! Someone, stop me!"

Unit 3

Exercise 3.1

1 が/を "What type of movie would you like to see?"
2 が "I can't see the area ahead of me well because of the fog."
3 を "She is reluctant to talk about herself."
4 が "I couldn't understand what he was thinking."
5 が/を "We couldn't discuss the important issue after all."

Exercise 3.2

1 に "If there is any problem, please tell me right away."
2 と "Ms. Fujiwara became friends with Ms. Sato while in graduate school."
3 に "I emailed everyone, but I only got these replies."

4 と "I frequently had fights with my younger brother when I was a child."

5 に "My parents were strict with me."

Exercise 3.3

1 と "Though she married a Japanese national, her citizenship is Canadian."

2 を "The child looked at me intently."

3 に "At the police box, I asked a policeman for directions."

4 に "I ran into an old high school friend in downtown Tokyo."

5 と "Both my sister and I talk a lot with my parents at the dinner table."

Exercise 3.4

1 を **2** を, に/へ **3** を, Ø

Exercise 3.5

1 楽譜の読み方 **2** 先生の子供の扱い方 **3** 日本での英語の教え方

Unit 4

Exercise 4.1

お名前は、杉田さんでしたね。慶応大学の学生で、2年生でしたね。
出身は、新潟でしたね。専攻は、工学でしたね。

"Your name is Ms. Sugita, right? You are a Keio University student and a sophomore. You are from Niigata. You major is engineering, correct?"

Exercise 4.2

1 出す "Ms. Smith checked the *kanji* once more before turning in her composition homework."

2 乗る "The super express that I was going to get on arrived at the platform."

3 読んだ "Please return the newspaper that you have finished reading."

4 来る "I waited at the coffee shop until my friend came."

5 いる "I heard someone singing a song."

6 言った "I noticed my own error after complaining to them."

Exercise 4.3

1 前 "The car entered the intersection before the traffic light changed to red."

2 ながら "I listen to the radio while driving a car."

3 間 "All the time I was driving, my friend was asleep next to me."

4 間 "While I was sleeping, the car crossed the mountain ranges."

5 うち "Let's hide the presents quickly before the children wake up."

Exercise 4.4

着いた, 始まる, 待っている "Hello, where are you?" "I'm at a duty-free shop. Where are you, Midori?" "I've just arrived at the gate. You should hurry. First-class boarding is about to begin in a few minutes." "I'm OK. Don't worry. I am waiting at the register, but I will be done in a moment."

Exercise 4.5

1 ばかり "I just ate a little while ago, so I can't eat dinner yet."

2 ところ "I've just tucked all the clothes in my suitcase, and now I am taking a short break."

3 ばかり "The cell phone that I had just bought broke."

4 ところ "The movie ended with the scene where the two were finally reunited."

5 ばかり "I've just begun playing golf, so I am not good, you know."

Exercise 4.6

1 聞きながら新聞を読みます。

2 見ながら{掃除をします/掃除機をかけます}。

3 飲みながら{勉強します/本を読みます}。

Unit 5

Exercise 5.1

1 置かれる　置かれない　置かれた　置かれなかった

2 忘れられる　忘れられない　忘れられた　忘れられなかった

3 ひらかれる　ひらかれない　ひらかれた　ひらかれなかった

4 読まれる　読まれない　読まれた　読まれなかった

5 使われる　使われない　使われた　使われなかった

6 減らされる　減らされない　減らされた　減らされなかった

7 される　されない　された　されなかった

Exercise 5.2

1 ドラエモン(は) "Doraemon is loved by people all over the world."

2 この家 (が) "This house was built exactly 100 years ago."

3 ウイルス(が) "A virus was contained in the file that I downloaded." (= The file that I downloaded was infected by a virus.)

4 あの人(は) "Why is she called 'Teacher'?"

5 ボランティア活動(が) "Volunteer activities are organized in various localities."

6 例年より多い積雪量(が) "This year, a snow accumulation greater than the regular year's has been reported."

Exercise 5.3

1 を "My mother is teaching English in a high school."

2 が "Japanese is taught in Thai universities, too."

3 が, で "Is Japanese rice wine being consumed all over the world?"

4 が "It is being awaited for Rowling to announce a new novel."

5 が "It was the year 1800 when the White House was built."

Exercise 5.4

1 起こされた "I am sleepy because I was forced to wake up by a phone call when I was in bed this morning."

2 入れた "For breakfast I toasted bread and brewed black tea."

3 発行された "The first stamp in Japan was issued in 1871."

4 読んでいる "People all over the world are reading this book now."

5 注目されている "The American president is being closely watched by people all over the world."

6 設計された "The Guggenheim Museum was designed by Frank Lloyd Wright."

7 届けられた "A flower bouquet, a congratulation gift on the new store opening, was delivered from a business partner CEO."

8 使われていた, 使う "For packages sent to foreign countries, ships were used once upon a time, but nowadays most people use airmail."

Exercise 5.5

1 治った "I have finally recovered from the cold that I had for a long time."

2 届きました "A text message arrived from my husband who is at work."

3 壊された "The intercom at the entrance was smashed last night. The culprit is most likely a drunkard."

4 落ち "An oil stain does not come off easily, so it is a nuisance."

5 乾いた "Won't you please bring in the clothes (hanging on the line) because they have dried?"

6 乗せられて "Being forced to ride a pony, my younger brother cried."

7 止められた "Driving on the highway very slowly, I was stopped by a policeman."

8 育てられました "I lost my parents when I was young and was raised by my grandmother."

Unit 6

Exercise 6.1

1 これ、{召し上がりませんか/お食べになりませんか}。
"Would you like to eat this?"

2 必ず参ります。 "I will come over without fail."

3 お醤油、取ってくれますか。 "Will you get me the soy sauce, please?"

4 お醤油、取ってくださる？ "Would you get me the soy sauce?"

5 明日は、雨だろう。 "It will probably rain tomorrow."

6 さあ、行きましょう。 "Well, let's go!"

Exercise 6.2

1 (d) "What are you doing there?"

2 (a) "There are mushrooms growing here (of all the places)."

3 (c) "That's quite interesting."

4 (b) "So, there was such a hideous incident."

5 (f) "It's been a while, Mr. Yamaguchi."

6 (e) "Have you been doing well?"

Exercise 6.3

1 A (A uses a plain honorific form)

2 A (B uses a masculine first person pronoun)

3 B (A uses a masculine conversation particle)

4 B (B uses a polite ending)

5 B (A uses a brusque command form)

6 B (B uses a feminine exclamative)

7 B (B uses a feminine ending)

8 A (A uses a feminine conversation particle combination; in addition, B uses a masculine adjective)

9 B (A uses a brusque command form; B uses the combination of a て-form and the conversation particle よ)

10 B (B uses an honorific prefix whereas A does not)

Exercise 6.4

2B:　私がするわ(よ)。

3A:　そろそろ行くわよ。

4B:　5時ごろだろう。

5A:　疲れたでしょう？休んでよ。

Unit 7

Exercise 7.1

1 楽しい　**2** 晴れだ　**3** 元気だ　**4** インタビューだ　**5** 美しい
6 きれいだ

Exercise 7.2

1 どこですか。

2 何でしたか。

3 あの人、先生な{ん/の}ですか。

4 空気がとっても爽やかです。

5 そろそろ行く時間ですよ。

6 アイスクリーム(が)好きですか。

Exercise 7.3

1 な "Being in front of the station, the apartment building appears to be very convenient."

2 の "I live in an apartment building whose first floor is a grocery store."

3 の "I am scheduled to travel to the Kansai area for three days beginning next Tuesday."

4 な "Tomorrow is a day off, you see."

5 の "My understanding is that the rate at the hotels around that area is about ¥20,000 per night."

6 な "The biggest problem is that nobody said anything."

Exercise 7.4

1 Ø "I wonder if this cup is clean."

2 だ "This is a problem."

3 だ "I hear that it is also going to snow in Washington, DC, this week."

4 だ "It is simple, so even a child can use it."

5 Ø "It looks like it's going to rain hard over the weekend."

6 だ "I'm going to turn off the TV because it's time to go to bed."

Exercise 7.5

1 な "It looks like the moon is really beautiful tonight."
2 Ø "He is of course a graduate student."
3 だ "It is quiet here, and besides you can see the stars clearly at night."
4 Ø "The building's exterior is dirty, but its interior may be clean/ beautiful."
5 Ø "I received a gift of a scarf from a friend whose mother is a designer."
6 Ø "It is very warm even though it is December."

Unit 8

Exercise 8.1

1 洗っている　2 みがいている　3 寝ている　4 読んでいる
5 見ている

Exercise 8.2

1 (c)　2 (a)　3 (d)　4 (b)

Exercise 8.3

1 うん、買ってある。
   "Have you bought the plane tickets?" "Yes, I have."
2 うん、予約してある。
   "Have you reserved a rental car?" "Yes, I have."
3 ううん、まだ取ってない。
   "Have you gotten the tickets for the show?" "No, I haven't."
4 ううん、まだ調べてない。
   "Have you checked the maps?" "No, I haven't."
5 うん、読んである。
   "Have you read the travel guide?" "Yes, I have."
6 ううん、まだしてない。
   "Have you packed your suitcase?" "No, I haven't."

Exercise 8.4

1 消した　　　"I turned off the lights before going to bed."
2 消えた　　　"The candle went out because of the wind."
3 ぬらして　　"I wetted a towel and wiped my face."
4 壊れた　　　"The computer broke."
5 閉めて　　　"Please close the window."
6 直して　　　"I am repairing my computer."

Exercise 8.5

1 開^あいている "It's strange. The window is open."

2 かかっている "Because it's locked, I can't open it."

3 閉^しめてあります "I have closed the curtains. Please do not open them."

4 つけて "I can't see well. Please turn on the light."

5 かわかしています "Please wait a while for towels. I am drying them now."

Unit 9

Exercise 9.1

1 True 2 True 3 True 4 False

Exercise 9.2

1 たまねぎとねぎとにらとにんにくが嫌^{きら}いです。

2 (sample answer) ねぎとかにんにくが嫌^{きら}いです。
(You can use any two that Ms. Suzuki dislikes.)

Exercise 9.3

1 頼^{たの}んだり 2 誘^{さそ}ったり 3 調^{しら}べたり 4 泣^ないたり 5 立^たったり 6 壊^{こわ}したり 7 飛^とんだり 8 泳^{およ}いだり 9 掃除^{そうじ}したり 10 来^きたり

Exercise 9.4

1 (sample answer) 洗濯^{せんたく}(を)したり、掃除^{そうじ}(を)したりするのが嫌^{きら}いです。

2 (sample answer) スキーをしたり、外^{そと}でスケートをしたりするのが好^すきです。

3 (sample answer) レストランに行ったり、映画^{えいが}を見^みたりするのが好^すきです。

Exercise 9.5

1 消^きえたり "With red and green Christmas tree lights twinkling, the avenue in front of the station is really pretty."

2 なったり、なったり "The weather this winter is strange. It suddenly switches between warm and cold."

3 降^ふったり "The mountain top was cold. It rained one moment and in another moment it became foggy."

4 <ruby>飲<rt>の</rt></ruby>んだり "Because I don't like talking with people, I just eat and drink at a party."

5 <ruby>来<rt>き</rt></ruby>たり "Ms. Miyamoto travels back and forth between Japan and New Zealand on business."

Exercise 9.6

1 <ruby>風<rt>かぜ</rt></ruby>が<ruby>強<rt>つよ</rt></ruby>いし、<ruby>寒<rt>さむ</rt></ruby>い "Today, it's windy, and moreover it's cold. So, I will stay home instead of going anywhere."

2 <ruby>頭<rt>あたま</rt></ruby>が<ruby>痛<rt>いた</rt></ruby>いし、<ruby>熱<rt>ねつ</rt></ruby>がある "On top of a headache, I have a fever, so I will take a sick day off from school."

3 <ruby>日本<rt>にほん</rt></ruby>の<ruby>映画<rt>えいが</rt></ruby>が<ruby>好<rt>す</rt></ruby>きだし、<ruby>日本<rt>にほん</rt></ruby>の<ruby>文化<rt>ぶんか</rt></ruby>{は/が}<ruby>面白<rt>おもしろ</rt></ruby>い "I like Japanese movies. Moreover, Japanese culture is interesting. So I will major in the Japanese language."

4 <ruby>遅<rt>おそ</rt></ruby>いし、<ruby>明日<rt>あした</rt></ruby>(の<ruby>朝<rt>あさ</rt></ruby>)は<ruby>早<rt>はや</rt></ruby>い "It's late. Besides, we have an early morning tomorrow. So, let's excuse ourselves now."

Unit 10

Exercise 10.1

1 Bicycles must also stop.
2 Yield to an approaching car.
3 Curve ahead. Decrease speed.
4 Hard hat area. Do not enter.
5 Watch out. Do not come onto the road suddenly.

Exercise 10.2

1 たまには、<ruby>付<rt>つ</rt></ruby>き<ruby>合<rt>あ</rt></ruby>えよ。
2 もっと<ruby>食<rt>た</rt></ruby>べろよ。
3 からかうのはやめろよ。
4 これ<ruby>以上<rt>いじょう</rt></ruby><ruby>飲<rt>の</rt></ruby>むなよ。

Exercise 10.3

1 たまには、<ruby>付<rt>つ</rt></ruby>き<ruby>合<rt>あ</rt></ruby>いなさいよ。
2 もっと<ruby>食<rt>た</rt></ruby>べなさいよ。
3 からかうのはやめなさいよ。

Exercise 10.4

1 (d) 2 (a) 3 (c) 4 (b)

Exercise 10.5

1　中に入るな "I was told by the guard not to go inside."

2　もっと簡単に説明しろ "I was told by my teacher to give a more succinct explanation."

3　大きな声で話すな "I was told (scolded) by the guard not to speak in a loud voice."

4　一緒に行ってくれ "I was asked by Mr. Takahashi to accompany him."

Unit 11

Exercise 11.1

1　買いたい "The one that I want to buy if I have money is this model."

2　分かってほしかった "I wanted him/her to understand my feeling, but he/she did not."

3　行ってほしい "I want you to go with me. Do you have time?"

4　言いたい, 言ってほしい "If you have something you want to say, I want you to say it straightforwardly."

Exercise 11.2

1に, が　2が, に　3が, に

Exercise 11.3

1　何を作ってほしい？

2　どちらを見てほしい？

3　誰に会ってほしい？

4　何時に来てほしい？

Exercise 11.4

1　"Would you please tell me what you need?"

　　(a)　必要なものを言って頂けませんか。

　　(b)　必要なものを言って頂きたいのですが。

2　"Would you please read this document and make a comment?"

　　(a)　この書類を読んでコメントして頂けませんか。

　　(b)　この書類を読んでコメントして頂きたいのですが。

Exercise 11.5

1　(sample answer)先生、お忙しいところすみませんが、推薦状を書いて頂けませんか。

2　(sample answer)すみませんが、ここにお名前とご住所とお電話番号を書いて頂けませんか。

Exercise 11.6

1　to check off the items that apply on the check list
2　to email the checked list to Yamada at t-yamada@productservice.jp
3　to write "Q129HY" on the subject line

Exercise 11.7

"How to write emails effectively 1: If you want to make sure that the receiver of your email reads it promptly, write the subject line in such a way that they can understand the content just by reading it. Also write what you would like the reader to do clearly inside [ ] as in '[Please check] 11/3 schedule'."

Unit 12

Exercise 12.1

1　買おう "I am thinking of buying a new laptop. I wonder which model will be good."
2　帰ろう "I was thinking of going home early tonight, but it turned out to be impossible."
3　食べよう "Intending to eat it later, I put it away in the refrigerator."
4　聞こう "I thought of asking her name, but I couldn't."

Exercise 12.2

1　(e) "I thought of buying it once, but I decided not to because it was too expensive."
2　(f) "I thought of calling home, but because I became busy in the afternoon, I forgot about it."
3　(a) "I thought of going to bed early, but I could not complete the report."
4　(c) "Because it was cold, I thought of putting on a hat, but I could not find one."
5　(d) "I thought of watching the program from 8 o'clock, but the power went out shortly before."

Exercise 12.3

1 いつから留学しようと思っているんですか。

"I am thinking of studying in the UK." "Starting when?"

2 どんな仕事を始めようと思っているんですか。

"I am thinking of starting a new job." "What kind of job?"

3 いつ行こうと思っているんですか。

"I am thinking of going to Tokyo." "When?"

4 {どうして/なぜ}やめようと思っているんですか。

"I am thinking of leaving my current company." "Why?"

Exercise 12.4

1 いつしようと思っているの？

2 どこでしようと思っているの？

3 誰を呼ぼうと思っているの？

4 {何/どんな食べ物や飲み物}を出そうと思っているの？

5 どんなプレゼントを買おうと思っているの？

Exercise 12.5

1 会わない "Do you intend to see him?" "No, I don't intend to."

2 じゃなかった "Why did you sell your mother's ring?" "To tell you the truth, in the beginning I did not intend to sell it, but I desperately needed cash."

3 だった "Your homework has not been submitted, right?" "I am sorry, Professor. I intended to turn it in yesterday, but I forgot."

Exercise 12.6

1 どの国で販売するつもりですか。

2 いつから販売するつもりですか。

3 いくらぐらいに価格を設定するつもりですか。

4 古いモデルの販売を終了するつもりですか。

Unit 13

Exercise 13.1

1 見に 2 会いに 3 とりに 4 しに

Exercise 13.2

1 東京に行くのに(は)エコノミー・クラスでいくらかかりますか。

2 東京に行くのに(は)直行便でどの{ぐらい/くらい}かかりますか。

3 切符を買うのに(は)何が要りますか。

4 ワインの瓶を包むのに(は)何を使ったらいいですか。

5 搭乗手続きをするのに(は)どこへ行ったらいいですか。

Exercise 13.3

ため, に, ため, ため, の/ため

In Japan, in order to be admitted into a university, everyone takes an examination called the "University Entrance Exam Center Examination." This exam takes place in January every year, and many high school and preparatory school students come to (cities like) Tokyo and Osaka to take the exam. Hotels provide services such as serving special menus for such students and creating study spaces. It looks like it costs a lot of money to take the examination.

Exercise 13.4

1 (a) 会議に間に合うようにタクシーに乗りました。

"I took a taxi so as to be in time for the conference."

2 (c) かぜをひかないように毎日うがいをします。

"I rinse my mouth and throat every day so as not to catch a cold."

3 (e) お弁当を忘れないようにかばんに入れておきます。

"So as not to forget (to take) it, I am putting my lunch box in my bag."

4 (f) 先生の話がよく聞こえるように一番前の席に座ります。

"I am sitting in a front row seat so that I can hear the teacher well."

5 (d) 寒くないようにマフラーをして行きます。

"I am going out wearing a scarf so as not to be cold."

6 (b) 座って行けるように指定席を予約しておきます。

"I am going to reserve a pre-assigned seat so that I can travel seated."

Exercise 13.5

1 ように "I used special toothpaste so that my teeth will become white."

2 のに "For brushing your teeth, a soft brush is optimal."

3 ために "In order to make my teeth white, I brush them carefully every day."

4 のに "It takes about ten minutes to brush my teeth."

Exercise 13.6

1 (プリンターの)インクカートリッジを２つ注文しておいて(く
ださい)。
2 6時までにごみを出しておいて。
3 明日クラスで{話せる/ディスカッション出来る}ようにこの
新聞記事を読んでおいてください。
4 洗濯石けんを買っておいて。

Unit 14

Exercise 14.1

1 安くなる "become cheap"
2 よくなる "become better"
3 使わなくなる "stop using"
4 知りたくなる "feel like learning about it"
5 覚えやすくなる "become easier to memorize"
6 静かになる "become quiet"
7 大学生になる "become a university student"
8 雪になる "begin to snow"

Exercise 14.2

1 忙しく "I was not very busy before. However, I have become busy. I
am busy now."
2 寒く "It was not cold in the morning. However, it became cold in the
afternoon. It is cold now."
3 友だちに "We were not friends last semester. However, we became
friends this semester. We are friends now."
4 行きたく "I did not want to go to Japan before, but after studying
Japanese I became interested in going. I want to go very much now."
5 なく "There was a pay phone here, too, until a little while ago, but it
disappeared while I was not paying attention. There is no pay phone
anywhere now."
6 買いたくなく "I wanted to buy it before, but reading a review on it I
lost interest. Now I don't want to buy it at all."

Exercise 14.3

1 飲むように "Americans used to drink weak coffee in the past, but
since about 20 years ago they began to drink strong coffee."
2 するように "I started to make online purchases and stopped going to
department stores."

3 調べるように/見るように/知るように "After beginning to check the time on my cell phone, I stopped wearing a wristwatch."

4 (飛んで)来るように. "When I placed a bird feeder near a window, many small birds began to fly over."

Exercise 14.4

1 大学院に入学することになりました。

2 日本の会社{で働く/に就職する}ことになりました。

3 6月に結婚することになりました。

4 ロンドンに{引越しする/引越す/移る}ことになりました。

Exercise 14.5

1 咲くようになった "In the past cherry blossom bloomed in April every year in this region, but since about ten years ago, they began to bloom in March every year."

2 咲き始めた "I heard that the cherry blossom near the river started to bloom, so how about going to see them together on the weekend?"

3 読み始めて "OK, it's time to begin the test. Please begin reading the explanation on the first page."

4 見えて来た "We are arriving at the hotel soon. Look, we can see the ocean over there now."

Unit 15

Exercise 15.1

1 どうやら "Charcoal-black clouds are spreading across the sky. It looks like it is going to rain."

2 きっと "Please have confidence in yourself and do your best. I am sure it will turn out all right."

3 たしか "If I am not mistaken, Ms. Yokoyama is from Kobe."

4 たぶん "I cannot tell for sure, but probably it will be ready by tomorrow."

5 もしかしたら "There is a chance that Mr. Yoshida may not come."

6 どうやら "It seems like my prediction was inaccurate."

Exercise 15.2

1 Ø "I will rain tomorrow."

2 Ø "It may snow the day after tomorrow."

3 の "I understand that there will be a thunderstorm in the morning."

4 の "It seems like it is going to be cloudy in the afternoon."

5 Ø "It looks like we are going to have some nice weather over the weekend."

6 Ø "It looks like it will remain sunny till the end of next week."

Exercise 15.3

1 Ø "I suppose that Ms. Kuramoto's wedding will be luxurious."

2 Ø "The story may be famous in Europe."

3 な "I should be free on Saturday."

4 な "Ms. Jones seems to like *sushi*."

5 Ø "Professor Fujimura looks like he is in good shape."

6 Ø "It appears that you need at least ¥1,500,000."

Exercise 15.4

1 なる "We will have a big snowstorm tomorrow."

2 会議 "Tonight might be [a night for] a meeting."

3 静か "I suppose that it will also be quiet at night around here."

4 おいし "Wow, this cake looks good."

5 大変だった "I suppose it was tough last night because of the traffic jam."

6 買える "It seems like it's possible to buy TVs at very reasonable prices these days."

7 来られない "I am sorry, but I may not be able to come to the university tomorrow."

8 受からなかった "It appears that Mr. Kishida did not pass the entrance examination."

Exercise 15.5

1 (b) キムさんは学生だから、あまりお金がないはずです。

"Mr. Kim is a student, so I expect him not to have much money."

2 (a) ユーさんの専攻は日本語だから、日本語がよく分かるはずです。

"Ms. Yu's major is Japanese, so I expect her to understand Japanese well."

3 (d) ハリケーンが来るから、明日は大雨のはずです。

"A hurricane is on its way, so I expect it to rain heavily tomorrow."

4 (c) 高橋さんはテニスクラブのメンバーだから、テニスが上手なはずです。

"Ms. Takahashi is a member of a tennis club, so I expect her to be good at tennis."

Exercise 15.6

1　8時の授業に行くはずだったんですが、行けませんでした。
2　宿題を{終える/全部する}はずだったんですが、時間がありませんでした。
3　1時に友達に会うはずだったんですが、(友達は) 1時４５分まで来ませんでした。
4　テニスをするはずだったんですが、雨が降りました。
5　デートをするはずだったんですが、デートの相手が来ませんでした。

Exercise 15.7

1　あの先生は厳しそうだ。
　　"That teacher appears to be strict."
2　この映画はおもしろくなさそうだ。
　　"This movie doesn't appear to be entertaining."
3　あの人は学生のようだ。
　　"That person appears to be a student."
4　今度の土曜日は無理そうだ。
　　"Next Saturday does not seem to work out for me."
5　昨日は、雨が降らなかったようだ。
　　"It looks like it did not rain yesterday."

Unit 16

Exercise 16.1

1　と　"Mr. Hashimoto said that he would come by 4."
2　か　"Do you know where the professor is?"
3　と　"I think that the concert is from about 9."
4　か　"I forgot where I left my keys."
5　と　"My name is Yamazaki. It's nice to meet you."

Exercise 16.2

1　池田さんは阿部さんは車がないと言っていました。
　　"Mr. Ikeda said that Ms. Abe does not have a car."
2　ボブはハワイ旅行は楽しかったと言ったらしい。
　　"It appears that Bob said that he enjoyed his Hawaii trip."
3　道子はおいしいラーメンが食べたいと言っていた。
　　"Michiko was saying that she wants to eat delicious *ramen* noodles."

4 リーさんはインタビューはいつだったか尋ねました。

"Mr. Lee asked when the interview was."

5 シモナさんはお母さんはロシア人だと言いました。

"Simona said that her mother is Russian."

6 先生はお父さんはパリにいらっしゃるとおっしゃいました。

"My professor said that his father is in Paris."

7 井上さんに母は元気か聞かれました。

"I was asked by Ms. Inoue if my mother was doing well."

8 私は姉に子供の時よく近所の子供とけんかをしたと言われました。

"I was told by my sister that I used to have fights with neighborhood children when I was small."

Exercise 16.3

Ø, の, の, の, Ø

"Yesterday, I went to an Indian restaurant called 'Café Taj.' The *naan* there was delicious." "What's *naan*?" "It's a type of Indian bread." "Oh, you mean the thin bread. So where is that 'Café Taj'?" "It's in Shinjuku. It's on the third floor of a building named 'Mi Amore' right outside the subway station."

Exercise 16.4

1 お花見って何(のこと)ですか。

(c) "What's *ohanami*?" "It means going to see cherry blossom. We don't use it for other flowers."

2 ホッチキスって何(のこと)ですか。

(b) "What's *hotchikisu*?" "The English word for it is 'stapler.' In Japanese, we adopted the name of the inventor."

3 パリコレって何(のこと)ですか。

(d) "What's *parikore*?" "It is an abbreviation for 'Paris Collection.' Like *kaanabi* from 'car navigation,' for instance, the Japanese language has many words like this."

4 魔法瓶って何(のこと)ですか。

(a) "What's *mahoobin*?" "It means 'magic bottle' and stands for a container that can keep drinks warm."

Unit 17

Exercise 17.1

1 はじめて

"I hadn't noticed it on my own, but just a moment ago I noticed that poster for the first time after having my attention directed to it."

2 はじめに

"Well, then, we are beginning the test. Please write your name first."

3 はじめに

"I caught a cold first, and then all my family caught a cold."

4 はじめて

"When was the first time you went to Japan?"

Exercise 17.2

1 True "Until the 16th century, the Japanese had not produced guns."

2 False "Until Commodore Perry came to Japan, no Europeans had come to Japan."

3 True "Mt. Fuji has erupted but not in the past 300 years."

4 False "Human beings have not been to the moon."

Exercise 17.3

1 会うことがありますか。

"Do you ever see Ms. Watanabe?" "Yes, I do sometimes."

2 使うことがありますか。

"Do you use a dictionary sometimes even now?" "No, I don't at all."

3 することがありますか。

"Do you ever shop online?" "Yes, I do frequently."

4 映画を見ることがありますか。

"Do you watch a movie at a movie theater sometimes?" "Yes, I do sometimes."

Exercise 17.4

(sample answer) 携帯電話やテレビやコンピューターは見たことも使ったこともないし、聞いたこともない。

Mr. Maeda has not left the jungle in the past 30 years. Having built a hut with materials that he can acquire in the jungle, he is living alone. He sees a lot of animals, but he has never once seen a person. He has never written or received a letter. Of course, he has not seen or used a cell phone, TV, or computer. Nor has he ever heard about them.

Exercise 17.5

行って, はいて, 試して, 注文して, 飲んで, 召し上がって

Ms. Lee is staying with a host family in Yokohama now. Today Ms. Lee went to a Tokyo department store alone for the first time. After trying on a few pairs of shoes on the first floor of the department store, she went to the electronics shop on the sixth floor and tried the newest type of notebook computer. Since she became hungry around 2 o'clock, she went to the cafeteria on the eighth floor and ordered *sushi* and *udon* noodles in Japanese. On the way out, she heard clerks in the basement grocery area saying "How about trying this *sake*?" "Please have a bite," and so on.

Unit 18

Exercise 18.1

1 an embedded sentence   **2** an embedded sentence   **3** a conditional clause
4 a conditional clause

Exercise 18.2

Non-past form	たら-clause	ば-clause	と-clause
使う	使ったら	使えば	使うと
使わない	使わなかったら	使わなければ	使わないと
読む	読んだら	読めば	読むと
読むつもりだ	読むつもりだったら	読むつもりなら	読むつもりだと

Exercise 18.3

1 映画スターにメールを書いたら、次の日に返事が(返って)来た。
2 右にまがったら、友達の家の前だった。
3 日本語で話したら、発音がいいと言われた。

Exercise 18.4

1 もっと食べればよかった。
2 誰かに聞けばよかった。
3 会わなければよかった。
4 手紙を書かなければよかった。

Exercise 18.5

1 5時に起きられなかっただろう。

"Because my roommate woke me up, I was able to get up at 5. If my roommate had not woken me up, I would not have been able to get up at 5."

2 起きなければ、6時の電車に乗れなかっただろう。

"Because I got up at 5, I was able to get on the 6 o'clock train. If I had not gotten up at 5, I would not have been able to get on the 6 o'clock train."

3 6時の電車に乗らなければ、テストの時間に間に合わなかっただろう。

"Because I was able to get on the 6 o'clock train, I was in time for the examination. If I had not gotten on the 6 o'clock train, I would not have been in time for the examination."

Exercise 18.6

1 難しかったら/難しければ

"If this problem is difficult, please do it later."

2 使ったら

"When you are done with the dictionary, please return it here."

3 行ったら/行けば/行くと

"If you go to Japan, you will become much more proficient in Japanese."

4 飲むのなら/飲むつもりだったら

"If you intend to have a drink at the restaurant, you must not drive there."

5 飲んだら

"Once you have had a drink at a restaurant, you must not drive home."

Exercise 18.7

1 "If you hear a strange sound coming from the house of your neighbor who is supposed to be away, what would you do?"

Sample answers:

私だったら、警察に電話します。

"I would call the police."

私なら見に行きます。

"I would go (to the neighbor's house) to check."

2 "If the car you have been driving comes to a halt on a highway because of heavy snow, what do you think you should do?"

Sample answers:

車の中で待てばいいと思います。

"I think that you should wait in the car."

歩ければ歩いて帰ればいいと思います。

"I think that, if you can, you should walk home."

Exercise 18.8
1 朝電話(を)しても、夜電話(を)しても、家にいません。
2 何度電話(を)しても、出ません。

Unit 19

Exercise 19.1

1 "The perpetrator turned out to be that guy as I had originally suspected."
2 "After carefully examining the situation, I request that you send this plan back to the drawing board."
3 "In winter, going to a hot spring beats them all (even though there are other attractions that I have considered)."
4 "Should I choose barbecued meat? No, I want to eat *tempura* as usual after all."

Exercise 19.2

1 まだ "I am sorry. It's not ready yet."
2 もう "Really? They are already gone?"
3 まだ "She is still a baby. Her sleeping face is adorable."
4 もう "Since the ship left Japan, it has already been a week."
5 まだ, もう "Can you still eat? I can't eat any more."

Exercise 19.3

1 けど
"It's a little expensive, but how about buying a small amount?"
2 のに/けど
"Although I took the trouble of taking a detour to go see the Todaiji Temple, it was under repairs, and I could not get inside."
3 のに/けど
"Even though you made it for me, I can't eat it."

4 けど

"It's delicious, but don't eat too much."

5 のに

"There are people who only think of themselves despite the
fact that everyone else is experiencing hardships."

Exercise 19.4

1 今日は寒すぎる。

"It's too cold today."

2 宿題が多すぎる。

"I have too much homework."

3 相手チームは強すぎた。

"The opponent team was too strong."

4 あの人はモラルがなさすぎる。

"That individual lacks morality (to the extent that it is appalling)."

Exercise 19.5

1 アイスクリームを食べすぎてしまった。

2 お金を使いすぎてしまった。

3 コーヒーに砂糖を入れすぎてしまった。

4 パスタを(長く)ゆですぎてしまった。

Exercise 19.6

1辛　**2**言い　**3**飲みすぎて　**4**長すぎ,寝てしまった

Unit 20

Exercise 20.1

1 やめさせる

2 払わせる

3 勉強させる

4 持って来させる

Exercise 20.2

1 に　　"Let me go!"

2 を　　"We will send a hotel employee over there now."

3 に, を "We will have our chef cook this fish right now."

4 に　　"We let the children eat first."

Exercise 20.3

1 払わせて "Please let me pay."

2 休ませて "Please let me have a break here."

3 撮らせて "Please let me take a photo."

4 ご紹介させて "Please let me introduce him/her."

5 読ませて "Would you please let me read it?"

6 置かせて "Would you let me put down my luggage here?"

Exercise 20.4

1 "The line at the reception desk was long, and I was (made to feel) frustrated."

2 "I {learned/was forced to learn} a lot of things through this trip."

Exercise 20.5

1 直させた/直してもらった

"Because my computer crashed, I {had it fixed/asked to have it fixed.}"

2 ぬすまれて

"I had my passport stolen on my trip and had a stressful time."

3 起こされた/起こしてもらった

"Because I {was woken by my mother/had my mother wake me up} at 5 this morning, I made it in time for the flight."

4 持たせて

"Sorry for making you carry heavy luggage."

Exercise 20.6

1 泣かれて His child cried.

2 かけられて His child locked the door from inside the hotel room.

3 ぬすまれて His camera that he had in the rental car trunk was stolen.

4 とられて The restaurant's bill was exorbitant.

Exercise 20.7

Sometimes what is known as *yarase* becomes an issue in relation to TV programs. This word means that the production staff of a documentary program make show participants do something specific or ask them to say something specific in order to make the story interesting. They do this to quickly produce a story that makes viewers cry or to make the viewers laugh. I wonder if this is something that should be permitted. It makes me wonder."

GLOSSARY OF GRAMMATICAL TERMS

Accent—Prominence in a word in the form of loudness, length, pitch, or any combination thereof. In Japanese, accent is realized primarily by manipulating the pitch level. For example, the word くま "bear" in Standard Japanese is said to have first-syllable accent because its first syllable く is marked by a relatively high pitch.

Action verb—A verb that denotes an action, e.g. 食べる "eat" and 走る "run." The subject of an action verb might induce change but does not undergo a change of its own. For example, in the sentence こどもがおもちゃをこわした "The child broke the toy," こども "the child" only induces change in おもちゃ "the toy." (⇔ stative verb, change-of-state verb)

Adverb—A word that modifies a verb, an adjective, or another adverb, e.g. ゆっくり "slowly," よく "well," すぐに "soon," and やっと "finally." An adverb does not conjugate.

Adversity passive—A type of passive construction in which the subject is emotionally affected by someone else's action, e.g. 父にボーイフレンドからの手紙を読まれた "I was negatively affected by my father's reading a letter from my boyfriend." Adversity passive sentences do not necessarily have active counterparts.

Agent—An active participant who initiates and carries out the action. For example, in both こどもがコップをこなごなにわった "The child broke the cup into pieces" and コップがこどもによってこなごなにわられた "The cup was broken into pieces by the child," こども "the child" is the agent.

Aspect—Characterization of an event in terms of how it flows in time without reference to its position in time. For instance, the endings 〜ている and 〜てある mark continuative aspect.

Auxiliary adjective—A form that conjugates like an い/な-adjective, but does not stand alone and adds a supplementary meaning to another predicate, e.g. ようだ in 雨が降ったようだ "It appears that it has rained."

Auxiliary verb—A verb that is used with another verb and adds a supplementary meaning. In the sentence, 父が自転車を直してくれた "My father fixed the bicycle (for me)," くれる acts as an auxiliary verb that adds the sense that the action was beneficial to the speaker.

Change-of-location verb—A verb that describes a change of location of its subject, e.g. 行く "go" in 銀行へ行った "I went to the bank."

Change-of-state verb—A verb that describes a change in its subject's condition, e.g. the verb こわれる "break" in せんぷうきがこわれた "The fan broke" (⇔ action verb, stative verb).

Compound adjective—An adjective that is formed by combining two or more words, e.g. 見つけにくい "hard-to-find."

Compound verb—A verb that is created by combining two or more words, e.g. 食べすぎる "overeat."

Conditional—A grammatical form or structure that expresses the notion "If X, then Y." For example, 晴れたら、行きます "If the weather clears up, we will go" is a conditional sentence.

Conditional clause—A dependent clause that sets the conditions for an action, decision, or judgment. Japanese has multiple conditional clause types, for example 〜たら, 〜ば, 〜なら, and 〜と.

Conjugation—Changes in the form of a predicate that reflect changes in its meaning in terms of tense, negation, number, and so on.

Connective—An independent word that connects two sentences, e.g. しかし "however" and だから "therefore."

Copula—A linking verb that is largely devoid of meaning of its own, e.g. だ in 田中さんは医者だ "Mr. Tanaka is a doctor."

Counter—A suffix to a number that is used to count things and events, e.g. 人 in 3 人 "three people" and 冊 in 3 冊 "three books."

Counterfactual condition—A hypothetical condition that is known to the speaker to be untrue. For example, もっと時間があったら、できるんだけど "If I had more time, I'd be able to do it" (⇔ factual condition, hypothetical condition).

Dependent clause—A sentence-like unit that is dependent on some other units in the sentence, such as the noun-modifying clause 田中さんがくれた in 田中さんがくれた本 "The book that Mr. Tanaka gave me," and the nominalized clause お皿を洗う in お皿を洗うのは好きじゃない "I don't like washing dishes" (⇔ main clause).

Direct quotation—Verbatim reproduction of the original utterance, such as 田中さんは「明日もう一度伺います。」と言っていた "Mr. Tanaka said 'I will come again tomorrow'" (⇔ indirect quotation).

Discourse—A structural unit of language that is larger than a sentence.

Disjunctive connective—A connective that connects two contrasting sentences, e.g. のに "even though" and けど "although."

Estimation form—A form that indicates the speaker's estimation of the likelihood of an event, e.g. かもしれない "there is a chance" in 明日は雪かもしれない "It might snow tomorrow."

Eventive verb—A verb that denotes an event that takes place at some point in time (⇔ stative verb).

Exclamative—A form or structure that is used to express the speaker's attitude or emotion, e.g. わあ "Wow" and なんてばかな！ "How ridiculous!"

Factual condition—A condition that led to a certain event in the past, as in the case of 家に帰ったら in 家に帰ったら、荷物が届いていました "when I returned home, (I found out that) a package had been delivered" (⇔ counterfactual condition, hypothetical condition).

Five-row verb—A class of Japanese verbs that appear with one of the five syllable types (i.e. *a, i, u, e, o*-row syllables), such as 書く "write" (e.g., *kakanai, kakimasu, kaku, kake, kakoo*) (⇔ one-row verb).

Honorific—A form of a verb, noun, or pronoun that expresses social distance or hierarchy by raising the status of a respected individual, e.g. いらっしゃる "come (honorific)" and 息子さん "son (honorific)."

Humble—A form of a verb, noun, or pronoun that expresses social distance by lowering the status of the speaker, e.g. 参る "come (humble)" and 愚息 "my son (humble)."

Hypothetical condition—A condition whose probability or outcome is not known to the speaker (⇔ counterfactual condition, factual condition).

い-adjective—A class of adjectives whose dictionary forms end with い, e.g. かわいい "cute" (⇔ な-adjective).

Imperative form—A verb form that is used to give an order, e.g. 来い "Come!"

Indeterminate pronoun—Japanese words such as 誰 and 何 that combine with particles も or か to create English counterparts of "anyone" and "something," etc.

Indeterminate quantifier—Expressions of quantity that are formed by combining the indeterminate pronoun 何 with a counter, e.g. 何人 "how many."

Indirect quotation—A restatement of the original utterance by the speaker, as in the sentence 田中さんは、来週もう一度僕に会いに来ると言っていた "Mr. Tanaka said that he will come again next week to see me" (⇔ direct quotation).

Internal process verb—A verb that expresses the speaker's internal thought, e.g. 思う "think."

Intransitive verb—A verb that that has a subject but not an object, e.g. 走る "run" and 寝る "sleep" (⇔ transitive verb).

Level of speech—Linguistically marked level of formality of a situation, most commonly by the distinct paradigm of conjugations and special vocabularies.

Main clause—A clause that can constitute a sentence on its own (⇔ dependent clause).

Mora—A basic rhythmic unit in Japanese. For example, とんぼ "dragonfly" has three moras, and 学校 "school" four moras.

な-adjective—An adjective that ends in な before a noun, e.g. 静かな "quiet." With the copula verb だ, it conjugates similarly to the noun predicate (⇔ い-adjective).

Nominalizer—An element that turns a sentence into a noun phrase equivalent. For example, の in テレビを見るのが好きです "I like watching TV" and こと in 私の趣味は料理をすることです "My hobby is cooking."

Non-subject agent particle —The particle に that marks the non-subject agentive phrase, as in the sentence ケンが先生にしかられた "Ken was scolded by the teacher."

Noun phrase—A unit that consists of a noun or a noun with a modifier, such as あの煙突のある大きな家 "that big house with a chimney."

Numeral quantifier—A word that consists of a counter and a number that indicates a quantity of things or events, e.g. 3 人 "three people" and 3 回 "three times."

Object—A noun phrase that is required by a transitive predicate, e.g. ケーキを "a cake" in 太郎はケーキを食べた "Taro ate a cake." or 数学が "mathematics" in 花子は数学が嫌いだ "Hanako hates mathematics."

One-row verb—A class of Japanese verbs that appear uniformly with *i*-row or *e*-row syllable before conjugational suffixes, e.g. 起きる "wake up" (e.g., *okinai, okimasu, okiru, okiro, okiyoo*) (⇔ five-row verb).

Particle—An element that appears after a noun or another particle to mark the function of the preceding part, such as が (subject) and は (topic).

Personal pronoun—A type of pronoun that substitutes for a noun or noun phrase that refers to people, e.g. あなた "you" and 私 "I."

Plain—A form or style that is unmarked and does not carry politeness information, e.g. 読んだ "I read it."

Polite—A form or style that is used to show the formality of a situation or the respect for others, e.g. 読みました "I read it."

Potential form—A form of a verb that expresses that someone is capable of doing something or that some action is possible, e.g. 読める "can read."

Predicate—A necessary component of a sentence that describes the action or state of its subject.

Progressive construction—A construction that expresses an on-going action.

Pronoun—A class of words used as substitutes for nouns and noun phrases, such as 彼 "he," それ "it," and の "one" in 青いの "the blue one."

Quotative particle—A particle used to quote an utterance either directly or indirectly. The quotative particle と is pronounced as って in informal speech.

Resultant continuative—A type of aspect that focuses on the end point of a change rather than the process.

Sino-Japanese—A Japanese word that originates in Chinese, e.g. 試験 "examination."

Stative predicate—A type of predicate that denotes a state (conditions, attributes, etc.), including stative verbs, noun predicates, and adjectives.

Stative verb—A verb that denotes a state of something or someone at some point in time (⇔ eventive verb, action verb, change-of-state verb).

Stem form—A tenseless form of a predicate, such as 食べ "eat" used in a variety of grammatical contexts including before ます.

Subject—A noun phrase that plays a primary role in a sentence. It often corresponds to an actor in an event or to a carrier of attributes. For example, in the sentence こどもがコップをわった "The child broke the cup," こども "the child" is the subject. In the sentence コップがわれている "The cup is broken," コップ "the cup" is the subject.

Suffix—A dependent element that attaches to the end of other words to form new words, e.g. さ "-ness" in やさしさ "kindness."

て-form—A form of a predicate that ends in て or で and is used to connect close attributes or closely related events, e.g. 食べて "eat" and かわいくて "cute."

Tense—The indication of time, such as present, past, or future.

Topic—A part of a sentence that is not in focus but rather provides a link to the previous discourse to clarify what is being talked about. In Japanese, the topic is typically marked with the particle は.

Transitive verb—A verb that relates two entities and requires a subject and an object, e.g. 食べる "eat" in 私はハンバーガーを食べた "I ate a hamburger" (⇔ intransitive verb).

Verbal noun—A noun that denotes an event or a state and is used as a noun or forms a compound verb with the verb する, e.g. 勉強 "study."

Volitional form—A form of a verb that expresses a voluntary intention, e.g. 行こう "let's go."

Volitional subject—A grammatical subject that denotes an entity with a will.

Volitionality—A property of the grammatical subject regarding whether or not it has the will or volition to act.

Wh-question—A question that contains an information seeking word, e.g. 誰 "who" and 何 "what."

Yes-no question—A question that can be answered with yes or no.

INDEX